Mike & Linda,

Hope you enjoy my book &
find it helpful.

Al

When
LIFE
Strikes

Weathering Financial Storms

Cal Brown, CFP®, MST

Brown Books Publishing Group
Dallas, Texas

When Life Strikes
Weathering Financial Storms

Brown Books Publishing Group
16250 Knoll Trail, Suite 205
Dallas, Texas 75248
www.brownbooks.com
(972) 381-0009

ISBN: 978-1-61254-032-0
Library of Congress Control Number: 2011937531

Printed in the United States of America
10 9 8 7 6 5 4 3 2 1

To my mother, Louisa Brown, who wrote her first book when I was a teen, showing by example that writing a book is quite possible, as she went on to write three more. She has been my biggest fan since Little League, and had the most significant spiritual impact on my life.

To my wife, Charlyn, who insisted on coming after my mother in this dedication, for all of the love, the encouragement, the happiness and laughter, and the endurance of everything we've been through together. She has encouraged me to take risks and pursue my dreams, and was excited and "on board" with this book project from day one.

To our boys, Chavis, Ryan, and Manuel, for contributing to the "life strikes" in our own family so that I could grow wiser and be better able to write this book (just kidding, boys . . . or not). You have brought tremendous joy to our lives and it is gratifying to see how well each of you, along with wives Marianne (Ryan) and Yanni (Manuel), are finding your respective directions in life while enduring "life strikes" of your own.

Finally, to everyone, family, friend, and client, who permitted me to use their personal stories and life lessons to provide the reader with greater insight along with the practical instruction and resources. I am grateful to each of you.

Contents

Part 6: What If I Lost My Identity?

Part 7: What If I Lost My Health?

Part 8: What If I Lost My Mind?

Acknowledgments

I would like to thank those who made this book possible:

Glenn Kautt, president and CEO of The Monitor Group, who has mentored and encouraged my professional growth. From achieving my master's of science degree in taxation, appearances on news programs, authoring professional and consumer-oriented articles and white papers for publication, to serving as president of the National Capital Area's Financial Planning Association and especially the writing of this book, he has been a fully vested supporter.

The members of my advisory board, who took their role seriously and were constructively critical and creatively inspiring as they assisted me in important decisions regarding this book: Cindy Gunn, Mike Hoover, Jeff Saylors, and my wife, Charlyn.

Special thanks to Lawrence Ineno, who persuaded me to get started with this book and whose collaboration and expertise have been invaluable to this project.

Why?

Paul was thirty-six and doing well in his career. He had enough income that his wife could comfortably stay home to raise their four children. We all know that at times "life strikes," and by the time his cancer was found, it had spread throughout his lymph nodes and eaten away at his body. He and his family were unprepared for this sickening discovery, and a frantic chase for a cure was all this couple had time for during the pain-filled final six months of his life.

Morgan was forty-eight, a bright, successful career woman and married mother of two young adults. She was a new grandmother and life was good. She wanted her body to reflect the vitality of her life, to look its best. She went for routine cosmetic liposuction, then life struck, and she died on the operating table. Her husband lost his vibrant, beautiful wife, her daughters their best friend, and the grandchildren their Grandma.

When life strikes, it comes out of nowhere, hits hard, and leaves devastation in its path. The worst strikes come from the death of a loved one, but life strikes in many other ways as well. We can lose our marriages, our careers, our investments, and our physical and mental health. We can even have our identities stolen. When the strikes come, they affect all who are not sheltered—the spouse, the children, the business partner, the invalid parent.

We all wish to hang onto our delusions of immortality and security for as long as we can. We want to believe that death will come in proper order and at a proper time after we have lived a long life, made a successful career, enjoyed a happy marriage, and watched our children grow and our grandchildren graduate. We plan our retirement full of recreational activity and travel, but life strikes when we least expect it and in ways we cannot fully anticipate.

Careful planning provides the only protection we can truly give to ourselves and is one of the greatest gifts we can give our loved ones. By preparing and planning ahead, we can make difficult decisions now, when we have time, clarity, health, and resources for contemplating the possibilities. For the ultimate strike—the loss of life itself—our preparation will make it easier for our loved ones when we cannot be there to help. In other areas, our careful planning can avoid pitfalls, save money, overcome obstacles, and make the most of the time and resources we have.

It is natural to worry about our health, our careers, and even about what will happen to us after the death of our loved ones.

One day I stopped by my brother's house for a bite to eat after visiting a client in the area. My sister-in-law, Teresa, surprised me by asking, "What if Jack died? What would I do?"

"You'd call me," I told her.

"But what if I didn't have enough money to be one of your clients?"

"Teresa, you're my brother's wife," I replied. "You'd call me and we'd help you."

Then she said something that caught me off guard again. "Well, what about everyone else? What would they do?"

Exasperated, I answered, "I don't know! What do you want me to do?"

"You should write a book," she said. "And then you should get on Oprah!"

"OK, Teresa, I'll get right on that."

My sister-in-law's what-if was one of thousands of similar questions addressed to me during more than a quarter century of helping people plan their financial lives. Collectively they fall into fewer than a dozen financial quandaries or life challenges. As I continued to deal with clients and their life challenges, my sister-in-law's concern, frustration, and comments stayed with me.

You see, I am a wealth manager working with those who have been blessed with much. Life strikes everyone, though, regardless of their financial blessings. My sister-in-law needs the same assistance as my wealthiest client, because she will deal with many of the same life events. We all go through major events that can turn our lives upside down, and when they do, we all need answers to life's pressing questions. My own life is a perfect example, and I am by no means unique in this:

1983: My career in logistics/transportation (my college major) ended with the drop in oil prices and the deregulation of certain government entities; all the expertise, certifications, and professional designations I had earned were no longer of value. I changed careers to financial planning.

1988: My first marriage ended in divorce.

1995: My parents lost their house to Hurricane Opal.

1996: My father died unexpectedly at age sixty-nine.

1996: The week after Christmas, my youngest brother, only thirty-six years old, died unexpectedly, leaving a wife and three young children.

1997: I was in Chicago at my brother's funeral, and my second wife was in Ohio at her grandmother's funeral. My wife had lived much of her early years with her beloved grandmother, who was 101 and had been in a nursing home for several years.

1999: I had triple bypass surgery.

2004: My wife had double bypass surgery and experienced collapsed lungs.

2006: My wife's mother came from Ohio to live with us because she suffered from acute dementia.

2008: My wife's mother died in our home.

2010: My son, at age twenty-five, buried his mother, who was my ex-wife. She died unexpectedly at age fifty-eight and he became executor of her affairs.

2010: My mother experienced renal failure and almost died. The process of decision-making for her continued care and safety has been put into motion and is impacting the lives of her three living sons and their spouses. This situation is still unfolding.

As we go through life, we are sometimes struck by the unexpected. Even those who expect challenges can still be caught off guard because reality is different from what was anticipated. "Life strikes" are similar to lightning—at times we see clouds on the horizon and expect a storm, yet when and where the storm strikes and how great an impact it will have remains unpredictable. Sometimes there is no warning and the strike is quick and powerful, and it is not until after the strike has passed that the damage can be seen. The impact of the strike may extend well beyond the initial destruction, and the ripple effect may go on for years, testing our financial, physical, and emotional endurance.

I can help you plan for these occurrences using generalized planning processes and strategies, but you should be aware that whatever is planned is subject to the unique timing, intensity, and duration of that event in your life and your specific set of circumstances. This book is not a "do-it-yourself" guide; rather, it is a starting point for making good decisions. In many cases, you will first want to educate yourself by reading this book and then go to a professional advisor for his or her expertise. Some things you may be able to do yourself, but for others it is in your best interest to get an expert on your side. Just as with car repairs or home maintenance, there may be some tasks that are within your skill set, but trying to fix other problems will only leave you frustrated—and you may have to hire someone to fix the original problem plus whatever you broke during your attempt to go the cheap route.

When Life Strikes is the result of determining the eight most common crises or life cycles that I have helped my clients navigate through the years. These life strikes will universally impact everyone at some point, and to some degree, during their lifetime. No one is exempt!

How to Benefit Most from This Book

I recently read a letter to *Reader's Digest* from a man who said his mother had died, followed a few months later by his wife, and then he lost his job, his house, and ultimately went bankrupt—all in one year! The good news is that life usually does not strike with all its many crises at one time, as with this man. Therefore, it is not necessary to read this book cover to cover. Read only what is pertinent for you at this time.

Because financial planning is my area of expertise, *When Life Strikes* is primarily a guide to the most common financial cycles and crises in life, giving sound financial guidance and useful information above all else. However, I have had the privilege of working with countless clients in a wide spectrum of challenging life situations, and I have learned from their experiences. This book will go beyond financial know-how, as it is meant to help you prepare in a variety of ways for the inevitable and deal with the unexpected when it occurs. You will want to read the chapters that are relevant for prudent planning of your successful journey through the cycles of life, and when a crisis impacts you or your finances, pick up the book again and use it to help you deal with whatever unexpected crisis is occurring in your life at that time.

When Life Strikes is a unique combination of real-life stories juxtaposed with rather technical topics. In order to let the stories flow and not get "bogged down" with definitions and terminology, I have created a glossary of sorts at the back of the book, called the Financial Toolbox. If you see a term in **boldface**, this indicates that the topic is explained more fully in the Financial Toolbox and you can refer to that section for additional information.

Each issue discussed in this book has two aspects: planning ahead and dealing with reality. In most cases, the issue is divided into two chapters, the first dealing with plans or preparations and the second with advice for facing a crisis that has already struck. Chapters 7 and 10 include both aspects in a single chapter.

Every story you read in this book is true. If it pertains to me or my family, it is identified as such. However, if it is a story about someone else, I have changed the names of the people involved. The stories are true, but their names are fictional.

Whether planning for or dealing with a crisis, it is my sincere hope that this book will provide direction to help position you for success and assist you in getting past the crisis at hand. While money can solve many problems, it cannot insulate even wealthy families from horrendous life strikes. All of us desire a stable, secure, peaceful, calm, and comfortable financial life, but again, none of us are exempt from these various crises. *When Life Strikes* is a resource that will help you prepare and work through these unpleasant but inevitable life events.

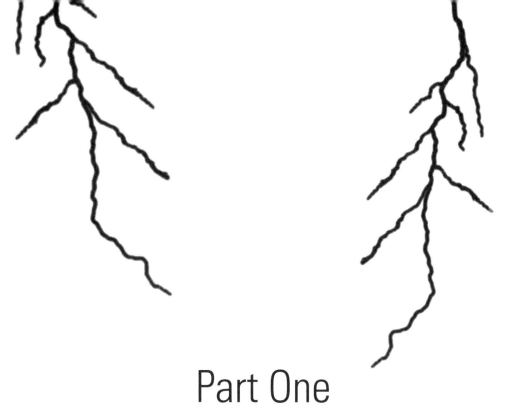

Part One

What If I Lost My Spouse?

Chapter 1

Preparing for the Worst

And inasmuch as it is appointed for men to die once . . .
—Hebrews 9:27

Hurricane Opal began her dance out in the Gulf of Mexico, swirling slowly at first. Then with delirious, chaotic fervor she began to order the grim, dark shape of her body, spinning and spinning, forming herself into an unholy mass and teasingly listing to and fro until she ran, full force ahead, directly at my parents' home in Pensacola Beach, Florida. Life struck—Opal flattened their home, but they were safely off the island. When they were allowed back, they appeared on *The Today Show* and *Good Morning America* sitting in Dad's favorite chair on the sugar-white sand with the wreckage of their house behind them.

They began the terrible process of recovering from the loss of their lifelong collection of mementos, which had graced their home after forty-six years of married life. Then they started negotiating with insurance companies and building contractors with stricter structural laws and the new "hurricane-proof" designs required to rebuild their home. There was the search for temporary shelter as their home was rebuilt. Together they worked through each detail until that summer day when a lightbulb went out in the little condo that was their temporary home. My mother climbed up on the ladder with the lightbulb while my father held the ladder firmly in place with his left hand (life had struck him at birth, shriveling his right arm). My mother was looking up at the ceiling fixture and screwing in the bulb when she heard an impact. Life had struck again—my father had died instantly of a heart attack. He had carefully planned his estate in the event of his death, but who could have anticipated the double strike? My mother would carry on alone.

Losing a spouse is one of the worst life strikes imaginable, and it can happen at any time to any married couple. The loss of a spouse leaves behind a wake of emotional despair that is further complicated by complex financial obligations. However, advance preparations can make a world of difference for the loved ones left behind. In this chapter, I will guide you through ways to plan ahead. By the end, you'll understand how to protect yourself and those you love.

Planning Ahead

"Cal, my husband is dying of cancer," my client told me. Joan and Patrick had been married for only three years when terminal illness struck. Sadly, Patrick's doctors told them that he would most likely not make it to their fourth anniversary. The couple was in their late fifties and had no children.

Three years prior, Joan had phoned me and shared that she was engaged to the love of her life. As her Certified Financial Planner® professional, my first impulse was to ask, "How are your estate documents and **titling**? We should probably review your need for **life insurance**, power of attorney, **revocable living trust**, and **advance medical directive** . . . and that's just to start." Thankfully, my genteel upbringing triumphed, and I began by congratulating her instead.

I didn't wait long to encourage the newlywed couple to plan for the future. From the beginning of their marriage, I urged them to create a living trust. That's where we hit a roadblock—one that would take years to fix.

In the following sections, I'll describe the pitfalls that Patrick and Joan faced so that you can avoid the considerable costs and stress that they experienced.

Five Essentials that Will Prepare You for the Worst

When a spouse dies, the more you've prepared ahead of time, the more likely you'll be able to make wise decisions despite enormous emotional distress. The following five building blocks must work together in order to create a financial foundation that will support you during difficult times:

- Trusts
- Wills
- Durable power of attorney
- Advance medical directive
- Life insurance

Trusts

Patrick owned a successful business and retained a corporate attorney who was his chief legal counsel. The lawyer wasn't

> A living trust is a legal contract that provides for the management and transfer of all assets titled to it. The "living" in living trust means that the trust was formed while the person was still alive. There are revocable and **irrevocable trusts**.

a specialist in estate planning, but this didn't stop her from providing estate planning advice to her client.

"Cal, my attorney says that I don't need a living trust," Patrick told me during one of our meetings.

I'm always astounded when attorneys advise their clients that living trusts aren't necessary. I asked Patrick if his lawyer gave him a reason.

"Because **probate**'s not that bad," he said.

The last thing I want to do is to criticize lawyers (my father was an attorney). The reality is that I couldn't do my job without collaborating with estate planning attorneys. But in Patrick's case, his corporate lawyer was advising him about an area that was outside her expertise. That would be like meeting with a podiatrist and asking him to diagnose your heart condition. In fact, the last time Patrick's lawyer was exposed to the technical aspects of estate planning might have been decades ago when she took one course in law school.

Despite doing my best to convince Joan and Patrick that they both needed a living trust, my initial attempts were unsuccessful—but I refused to give up because I knew that it was *absolutely essential* to their financial well-being. I worked with an estate planning attorney to convince them that probate was, in fact, *really bad*. Quite a while later, Patrick and Joan finally took my advice, at which point I arranged for the estate planning attorney to meet with them. The lawyer drafted their wills, living trusts, powers of attorney, and advance medical directives, but before we could move to the next important step—retitling assets—Patrick was diagnosed with cancer.

What Is Retitling Assets?

If you've bought or sold a car, you know that the title is your legal proof of ownership. Or if you were single and then married, you may have retitled your savings account in order to make it a joint one with your spouse. Changing the ownership (also called the "registration") of what you own is called retitling the asset. In the case of a home, a deed is attached to the property that legally designates who owns it. Once you have a living trust and decide that your home will be one of the assets within it, you have to change the title (registration) on the deed.

For example, Patrick and Joan (or their attorney) had to go to the county courthouse and retitle their house's deed from "Patrick and Joan Thompson tenants by the entirety" to "The Patrick Thompson Trust tenants by the entirety with The Joan Thompson Trust." The same went for each of their investment accounts. Some of their accounts they registered as joint tenants with rights of survivorship or as "The Patrick Thompson Trust tenants in common with The Joan Thompson Trust." Others, like Patrick's certificate of deposit, which he had before he married Joan, he retitled to his trust alone. As you can imagine, registering each of their assets was a time-consuming task.

Although the process requires effort, it's important to recognize that whether or not you have a living trust, your assets should be retitled at some point. If you don't take care of this before you die, your executor will be responsible for doing so afterward. I've witnessed how difficult it is for a husband or wife to register assets after his or her partner's death. The surviving spouse is left grieving *and* retitling assets, which makes an already stressful situation even worse. That's why I'm convinced that it's most effective and efficient to first create a living trust. Next, register your assets to the trust while both you and your spouse are alive. Many estate planning attorneys neglect to complete this important second step, so make sure it happens.

The Financial and Emotional Costs of Probate

As Patrick's health continued to deteriorate, the couple scrambled to reassign all of their assets to their trusts. This task was made even more challenging because Patrick's success as a businessman meant that he had a complex collection of investments. Unfortunately the retitling was incomplete when cancer took his life, which meant that several significant assets had to go into probate. Sadly, had the couple not waited so long to finally decide to create a living trust, the process would have been complete, and probate could have been avoided entirely.

Over the next three years, Joan had to pay an accountant and an attorney to settle Patrick's estate. Also, for each year the estate was in probate, Joan spent thousands of dollars filing income tax returns for the estate. This was another expense that could have been avoided had all the assets been registered to the trust. In the end, probate lasted longer than their marriage itself. Joan told me that it was one of the most difficult experiences that she had ever gone through.

This experience brings me back to Patrick's corporate attorney, who told him, "Probate's not that bad." She was wrong. It is *that bad.* The following are three reasons why:

1. **Probate is a waste of time.** On average, it takes one to three years for a will to complete the probate process, although I've heard of complex estates taking decades

to settle. In fact, the July 25, 2005, edition of the *Los Angeles Times* reported that a home in Orange County had been in probate since 1925—eighty years! That's an extreme example, but probate usually takes much longer than people expect.

2. **Probate is expensive.** You often have to hire an attorney, who can bill from \$100 to \$500 per hour. The deceased person's estate also will have to file income tax returns for each year the assets remain in probate.

3. **Probate compromises your identity.** All wills are public documents. That means that anyone can access your loved one's will and see who received what and how much.

Living Trust Pluses

As you can see, one of a living trust's main advantages is that it lets you avoid probate. Below are additional benefits.

Professional Management

Every trust names a trustee whose role is to manage the assets titled to the trust. During the *grantor's* life, the grantor is usually also the trustee and is often cotrustee with his or her spouse. The trustees are able to manage their revocable trust's assets without complications—it is as if there were no trust at all. In addition, the trustees do not have to manage the assets themselves; they can hire investment professionals to do that work. Professional or not, all trustees have a legal responsibility to act in the best interest of the beneficiaries.

> A grantor is the person who created the trust.

7

Management during Disability

Imagine that you or your spouse become mentally incompetent, comatose, or severely disabled. The cotrustee or successor trustee can seamlessly manage the trust for the grantor.

> An estate tax credit allows you to pass a particular amount of money to your heirs, tax-free. If you are married, the amount that you, as a couple, can pass down doubles.

An Estate Tax Credit Can Save You Millions of Dollars . . .

A trust can contain a subtrust within it called a "credit shelter," "bypass," or "family" trust, which preserves the **estate tax** credit of the spouse who dies first. If a married couple doesn't have this subtrust, the credit of the spouse who dies first could be lost forever. A tax law passed in December 2010 increased the credit amount to $5 million and preserves the credit of the first spouse to die without this special trust; however, this special provision does not let you avoid taxes on the growth of that amount. Nor does it preserve the credit if there is a subsequent marriage. Furthermore, this law does not change the situation in states that have a lower exemption amount. This law expires after 2012, unless extended by Congress. To be on the safe side, it's best to have a credit shelter trust.

. . . And Innumerable What-If Scenarios

A trust can prepare you for the particulars of your family, such as the following:

- **What if we both die and our children are minors?** A trust can describe when and under what conditions the children will receive income and the principal (the original sum) of the trust.

- **What if my children are adults but are irresponsible, immature, or both?** You can have so-called "sprinkling provisions" in your trust that specify that your children will not get the inheritance in one lump sum after you and your spouse die. Instead, the principal will be "sprinkled" to them over several years or decades. Or it could remain in trust for their entire lives, with distributions to them totally at the discretion of the trustee, based on conditions you stipulate.

- **What if I'm worried that my spouse cannot manage my wealth after I'm gone?** The successor trustee you name will manage the assets in the trust and provide your spouse with income during his or her lifetime.

- **What if my spouse gets married after I die?** Imagine that you want your children from your first marriage to be the ultimate beneficiaries of your trust rather than your spouse's new husband or wife. Your trust can put assets into a subtrust called a Qualified Terminable Interest Property Trust, or QTIP. In a QTIP, your spouse will receive all of the income of the trust during his or her lifetime, but after his or her death, the principal of the trust will be distributed to your kids or whoever you decide should receive it.

- **And more what-ifs.** Every family has its own special circumstances. The financial aspects of these can be addressed in a trust. There are "incentive trusts," "dynasty trusts," "generation-skipping trusts," and more, all of which serve to accommodate your specific needs. In addition, you can donate to charities via your trust.

How Difficult Is It to Create a Living Trust, and How Much Does It Cost?

If you've researched online, you'll see that there are do-it-yourself sites where you can draft your own trust. Although it sounds easy enough, the fact is that the process can be mind-numbingly complicated, and it's best to hire an estate planning attorney. As a rule, the higher your **net worth**, the more complex your trust will be. In most cases, expect to pay a few thousand dollars.

"Why is it so expensive?" you ask.

You may find cheaper offers. *But this is not an area where you want to cut corners.* A well-drafted estate plan is expensive because it takes into consideration your net worth, estate taxes, and multiple what-if scenarios, several of which I've already described. Remember that it can save your family hundreds of thousands or even millions of dollars in taxes and other needless expenses.

In addition, a sound living trust aligns with the other four estate planning fundamentals: your will, power of attorney, advance medical directive, and life insurance. As you can see, your living trust requires expert attention. That's why I recommend that you hire an attorney who specializes in estate planning. To find a competent lawyer in your area, visit the American College of Trust and Estate Counsel website at www.actec.org.

Wills

You've probably heard the term "last will and testament." The will refers to a set of instructions stating what should be done with a decedent's assets after he or she dies. Wills and probate work together. Probate is a legal process that makes sure the will is followed according to state law. Probating a will also means that the will is being officially verified. One critical role of a will is that it names guardians for children who are minors. For instance, if an eight-year-old boy has only one parent and he or she dies, the will can specify who will take care of him. No other legal document can do this.

A Will Is Not Enough

The term "pourover will" refers to the fact that properly coordinated wills (that is, coordinated with a revocable living trust) will have language that dictates that if certain assets were not titled to the trust prior to death, they will pour over into the trust after the will has gone through probate.

It's important to remember that the will is not the primary determinant of who receives your estate; in fact, it's the last resort. Things that take precedence over the stipulations in the will are jointly owned property, **beneficiary** designations in life insurance and retirement plans, and trusts. If one of those three things exists for any asset, it doesn't matter what the will says. The property will go to the joint owner or the beneficiaries—it will *not* go to people named in the will.

The will is used to transfer property when an asset doesn't have another legally mandated path to follow. Furthermore, some parts of your estate aren't even considered probate assets, which means that they won't be considered when the courts probate your will. These assets are transferred by other means. The two main methods are joint tenancy and contract. Joint tenancy means that two or more

> A beneficiary is a person or entity who is named as the inheritor of property when the property owner dies.

people are equal owners in an asset, such as a house. A contract names a beneficiary. The following are examples of nonprobate assets and how the proceeds (money) are transferred:

- **Jointly owned property.** For example, a house titled "joint tenants by the entirety" or a bank account titled "joint tenants with the rights of survivorship" means the surviving partner will automatically receive the proceeds. Joint property is not affected by the will.

- **Life insurance.** The proceeds will go directly to the beneficiary or beneficiaries named in the policy.

- **Individual Retirement Accounts (IRAs) and other qualified retirement plans such as 401(k), 403(b), Thrift Savings Plan, SEP, SIMPLE, 401(a) Profit Sharing Plan, and more.** Like life insurance, these proceeds will go directly to the named beneficiary or beneficiaries in the plan document or account application.

- **Revocable and irrevocable trusts.** The beneficiary or beneficiaries in the trust will receive the proceeds in the amount and at the times specified by the trust document. In your revocable living trust, you should name a successor (or contingent) trustee who would take over upon you becoming incapacitated. In the event that you become mentally incapacitated, you can either resign as trustee or the successor trustee can provide evidence that you're unable to take care of yourself. Resigning as the trustee is much simpler than if the successor trustee must prove your incompetence.

Let's say that in your will you state that you want your life insurance proceeds to pass to your daughter. Life insurance is *not* a probate asset. Therefore it won't even be on the list of assets that the court will use when they probate your will. If the beneficiary on the life insurance policy is someone other than your daughter, your daughter will not receive that money.

Durable Power of Attorney

This is a legal document that gives one person the power to act on behalf of another. It ensures that someone will watch after your financial affairs if you become incapacitated. The words "power of attorney" mean that the person you name as "attorney-in-fact" or your "agent" has the legal authority to do anything you can do. This person is usually your spouse or an adult child. An attorney-in-fact is bound by law to act only in your best interest. The word "durable" means that it is in effect at any time. In other words, no one has to prove that you are incapacitated.

In general, a power of attorney creates an agency relationship where you (the principal) delegate to another (the agent or attorney-in-fact) the authority to make decisions for you during your lifetime. A "durable" power of attorney remains valid and operative despite your subsequent mental or physical incapacity. All fifty states and the District of Columbia have statutes authorizing the durable power of attorney.

Without a power of attorney, relatives—even spouses—cannot simply take over the affairs of another person who becomes disabled, incompetent, comatose, or otherwise unable to manage his or her own affairs. Nor can they borrow money to pay for medical bills, withdraw money from the disabled person's IRA or other retirement plan, sell real estate or other assets to raise cash (if titled only in the name of the disabled person), borrow against a life insurance policy, step in to run a family business, or initiate a host of other activities. Furthermore, without a power of attorney, the spouse or relative must ask a court of law to appoint a "guardian" for personal affairs such as medical care, a "conservator" for financial affairs, or both. Unfortunately, this process can take months. When a guardian or conservator is appointed, the individual becomes a ward of the state, and the guardian or conservator may need to obtain the approval of the court to do anything.

A durable power of attorney must be in place *before* you become incompetent; once you are incapacitated, it's too late. A durable power of attorney is *revocable*, which means that it can be changed at any time. States do *not* have to legally accept a durable power of attorney. Nor do financial institutions like banks, brokerage firms (such as Merrill Lynch, Schwab, and TD Ameritrade, to name a few), and mortgage companies. Instead its use is based on custom. Therefore, a revocable living trust is also recommended, where assets are titled to the trust. (Please refer to the Toolbox explanation of revocable living trusts.)

Advance Medical Directive

In many states, an advance medical directive is a single document that is a combination of two documents: the living will and the health-care power of attorney. The **living will** is what authorizes someone to "pull the plug"—that is, to terminate your life under specific circumstances. The **health-care power of attorney** gives legal authority for someone to make all kinds of medical decisions on your behalf; it is a durable power of attorney drafted specifically for health-care decisions.

The rules dictating health-care powers of attorney and advance medical directives vary from state to state. For more information, see advance medical directive in the Toolbox.

In 1996 the US government passed the Health Insurance

Portability and Accountability Act, or HIPAA. It was intended to protect the confidentiality of medical records. Overall, maintaining a patient's privacy is a good idea. HIPAA has made hospitals and doctors very careful about who has access to medical records. In addition, health-care professionals abide by strict standards in terms of who is allowed to make decisions on behalf of patients who aren't able to represent themselves. For instance, imagine that a husband tells his wife that if he were diagnosed legally brain-dead that he would want to be taken off life support. Without a health-care power of attorney, however, his wife may not be able to fulfill his request. Meanwhile, the hospital is charging tens of thousands of dollars a day to sustain his life in a vegetative state.

My son recently experienced this. His mother, who was my ex-wife, was on life support. Thankfully she had prepared ahead of time and our son had medical power of attorney. Although it was a terribly painful decision to make, especially for a twenty-five-year-old, he was able to grant her wish to terminate life support.

Life Insurance

Many couples with young children choose to have one parent, usually the wife, quit her job in order to raise their kids full-time. When I meet with these stay-at-home moms, one of the biggest fears they express is, "What will I do if my husband dies?" No doubt it's a sensitive subject to discuss. A wife may believe that her husband's reluctance to purchase life insurance reflects a lack of concern for the family's well-being. Meanwhile, a husband may not want to devote time to pondering his mortality. Here's where my clients defer the difficult conversation to me. They know that as a **fee-only** CFP® Professional, I do not sell insurance; that is, I have no financial stake in whether or not they buy life insurance. Therefore they appreciate my objectivity.

Unfortunately too many in this country overlook life insurance. An August 2010 article in the *Wall Street Journal* titled "More Go Without Life Insurance" stated that "nearly 1/3 of US households have no life insurance coverage, the highest percentage in nearly four decades . . . about 35 million US households neither own their own life insurance nor are covered by employer-sponsored plans." This is despite the fact that, as the article points out, "prices of *term* insurance policies have dropped in recent years."

> Term is one type of life insurance.

I worked with a couple who recognized that life insurance was a must-have, and as a result purchased a $500,000 policy on David. David and Rachel had two kids. Prior to raising her children full-time, Rachel worked as a project manager. She had been out of the workforce for five years when David died of a stroke. Fortunately, his death benefit gave her options and freedom to make critical decisions without the urgency that came from being cash-strapped. In fact, she was able to continue her role as a stay-at-home mom, rather than having to seek work right away and put the kids in daycare.

As a CFP® Professional, I've witnessed grieving wives who can't make ends meet scramble to find new husbands. As a result, they swiftly remarry. These are less than ideal circumstances under which one should be looking for a soul mate, and the outcome is not always favorable to anyone, especially the kids. The bottom line is, I've never heard of a widow complaining that her husband had *too much* life insurance.

Social Security Is Not Just for Retired People

In addition to life insurance, Rachel was able to support her family with an additional income stream. Because of her husband's death, Social Security benefits extended to her kids and would continue to do so until they reached age eighteen. Both life insurance and Social Security enabled Rachel to raise her children in the same house and keep their college savings plans intact.

The Five Fundamentals Provide Freedom and Fulfillment

Living trusts, wills, powers of attorney, advance medical directives, and life insurance all work together to give you financial support when your spouse dies. Adding these to your overall estate plan will take time and money. Note that the higher your net worth, the more you'll need to depend on experts such as attorneys, CPAs, and CFP® Professionals. When tragedy strikes, every penny paid, second spent, and ounce of effort exerted will not only provide you financial benefit but a peace of mind that is priceless.

Now that we've covered planning, we're ready for the next step. In the following chapter, you'll learn how to deal with reality—what to do *after* your spouse dies.

Chapter 2

Continuing On

They that love beyond the world cannot be separated by it.
Death cannot kill what never dies.
— William Penn

A Financial Plan for Life after Death

Judy had recently lost her husband to colon cancer. Her best friend, who was my client, knew that Judy was worried about her financial future, so she suggested that Judy give me a call. She and I arranged to meet at my office the next week. When Judy took a seat in our conference room, I asked her what her biggest financial concerns were.

"Now that my husband's passed, I don't know how I'll pay the bills and the mortgage. I'm also worried that I won't be able to send my kids to college. And I'm horrified that I'm basically going to be a bag lady when I'm old," she said.

"Between you and your husband, who managed the family finances?" I asked.

Judy shared that she had deferred all money matters to her husband, George. The couple agreed that raising the kids full-time was enough responsibility for her, so George took on paying bills and balancing the accounts. Although the arrangement worked while he was alive, it ended up leaving her financially inexperienced. For example, when I asked her basic planning questions such as, "What are your assets and liabilities?" and, "Did George have a pension with a survivor benefit?" she had no idea. Although her financial IQ had atrophied from years of neglect, from our first meeting it was clear that Judy was an intelligent woman and motivated to take charge of her future. In this chapter, I'll explain how Judy and I worked together. It took us three years of hard work, but the happy result was financial independence. Through her example, you'll learn the essential money management steps you need to take after the death of a spouse.

Step 1: Gather Information

Throughout our initial meeting, Judy's body language clearly expressed how deeply her anxieties ran. Her hands trembled when she said that she didn't know how she'd pay the bills. Despite being only forty years old, she cried as she revealed her fear of not having a penny left when she eventually reached retirement age.

"I know how desperate your situation seems. But as unusual as this sounds, I see it as an opportunity that will benefit you and your kids," I said.

Judy looked at me with an understandable level of skepticism. "What do you mean?"

"I think you'll agree that most of your fears are rooted in the unknown. Once we shed some light on your present circumstances, I think many of your fears will dissipate," I said.

A related example is *In the Dead of Night* by Gambiro Bikkhu, which recounts the story of a man who was driving in the middle of nowhere late at night. Rather than fall asleep at the wheel, he pulled to the side of the road and took a nap. Loud noises outside his car woke him. The surrounding darkness filled him with uncertainty, and then he heard the thud of footsteps. He immediately turned on the headlights but saw nothing alarming.

I'm being completely irrational, he thought to himself, and he eventually fell asleep again.

Suddenly he heard the footsteps again, and this time he tried to start his car, but the engine refused to turn. The plodding footsteps drew closer, followed by another set of footsteps. He looked out the window and spotted an arm dangling beside his car. Then the most grotesque face he'd ever seen pushed up against his window. It stared at him with massive red eyes, and it was foaming at the mouth. The frightful sight caused him to pass out.

Hours later he woke up. It was morning, and when he stepped outside, he discovered that what he thought was an arm was really a tree branch that hung above his car. He saw hoof prints sunk deep in the muddy earth, and when he scanned further he saw a broken fence. The man then realized that the monster from the night before was really a cow that had escaped its enclosure and rubbed against his car.

In Judy's case, she needed facts to diminish her fear of the unknown. I started the process by giving her a homework assignment. I asked her to collect all statements that arrived in the mail and bring them to our next meeting. She arrived the following week with a folder filled with utility bills and bank statements. I noticed nothing from a credit card company, and I asked her about this.

"I think George did all of that online," she said.

"That's not a problem. You can print the statements off the credit card company's website," I said.

She was hesitant to respond. "The thing is, I've never done that before, and I wouldn't even know where to start," she confessed.

I described what she needed to do in order to gain access to her accounts. Together we contacted the financial institutions and told them that her husband had died. All of the banks required Judy to send them a certified copy of the death certificate.

Step 2: Determine Income and Expenses

Judy devoted the next three months to reviewing her credit card statements and her checkbook to determine how much she spent every month. Although she wasn't used to keeping track of her expenses, her fears motivated her. For Judy, it was a matter of financial life or death.

Since George was no longer generating income for the family, we needed to calculate Judy's current sources of money. I asked her whether she planned to return to work. She knew that she needed to be an emotional anchor for her kids, and she preferred to continue staying at home to support them—at least until the youngest child was well into elementary school.

"Will this be possible?" she asked.

"I can't say for sure. We need to know exactly how much you have, the amount of income you're generating, and how much you're spending," I said. The process of gathering this data would address her fears of becoming a bag lady in her old age and not being able to cover her children's college costs.

First, we calculated her assets and income sources, which included the following:

- Cash
- Investments
- Retirement accounts
- Personal property, investment property, or both
- Social Security for her children who were minors

Next, we determined her liabilities, such as the following:
- Credit cards
- Auto loans
- Mortgage
- Personal loans

In chapter 1, I explained how assets must be titled to the trust. If not, they will go into probate. Fortunately George's investment accounts were registered as joint tenants with rights of survivorship, which meant that the funds were transferred to Judy with no complications.

Step 3: Summarize Net Worth

Once we collected financial data and determined her assets and expenses, I input the information into a spreadsheet that provided an overview of Judy's financial state. Judy was pleasantly surprised when she saw everything laid out on one sheet of paper in a **net worth** statement. She really had no idea she had this level of net worth.

The net worth statement summary appeared as follows:

Net Worth Statement Summary
Prepared For George Sample
As of Tuesday, August 16, 2011

Account Number	Account Description	Account	George	Judy	Joint	Total
Liquid Assets						
Sample Checking	Bank of America Checking	Joint	$0	$0	$100,000	$100,000
		Sub Total:	$0	$0	$100,000	$100,000
Insurance						
Sample Insurance	Prudential; DB $500k	Client	$150,000	$0	$0	$150,000
		Sub Total:	$150,000	$0	$0	$150,000
Invested Assets						
Sample Brokerage	Schwab Brokerage	Joint	$0	$0	$1,950,000	$1,950,000
		Sub Total:	$0	$0	$1,950,000	$1,950,000
Tax-Deferred Assets						
Sample 401k	Fidelity 401k	Client	$1,200,000	$0	$0	$1,200,000
Sample Roth IRA	Schwab Roth IRA	Spouse	$0	$250,000	$0	$250,000
		Sub Total:	$1,200,000	$250,000	$0	$1,450,000
Other Assets						
Sample Land	Land in Florida	Joint	$0	$0	$100,000	$100,000
		Sub Total:	$0	$0	$100,000	$100,000
Personal Use Assets						
Sample Residence	123 Virginia Blvd.	Joint	$0	$0	$1,500,000	$1,500,000
		Sub Total:	$0	$0	$1,500,000	$1,500,000
Liabilities						
Sample Mortgage	123 Virginia Blvd; Bank of America; 15 yr fixed; 5%	Joint	$0	$0	-$250,000	-$250,000
		Sub Total:	$0	$0	-$250,000	-$250,000
		Grand Total:	$1,350,000	$250,000	$3,400,000	$5,000,000

The document allowed us to determine Judy's fiscal health. My job was to use the net worth statement as a guide to structure her investments in a way that would generate cash flow—in other words, income. Our goal was to have enough regular income to meet her immediate needs. In addition, her financial plan had to support her until the end of her life. If, for example, we withdrew too much from her **portfolio** in order to cover immediate expenses, we ran the risk of negatively affecting her retirement savings.

If Judy's expenses exceeded her income, she had three options:

1. **Make more money.** Usually this requires either finding a job or getting a better-paying job.

2. **Sell assets.** This may mean selling a home and buying a smaller one. Or perhaps there is some other real estate that is not generating sufficient cash flow or tax benefits.

3. **Reduce living expenses.** This obviously calls for spending less money.

When I provide these three options to my clients, they'll often say something like, "Cal, there's no way I can reduce my spending!"

I'll then review their budgets by scrutinizing each expense. More often than not, they can eat out less often, cut back on trips to the mall, or drive less expensive cars. If the thought of reducing expenses makes them cringe, I'll point them to option 1, which is "Make more money."

CFP® Professionals add value to their clients' lives by accurately evaluating their budgets and providing solutions with measurable results. You may think that you can take a do-it-yourself (DIY) approach and manage your money without expert support, and you may be right. However, this often leads to incorrectly assessing your current fiscal state, not handling your problems effectively, or both.

Step 4: Create a Financial Plan

I based Judy's financial plan on both her net worth statement and her responses to income and expense questions that I provided her. Although she was relieved to have a plan, I reminded her that life strikes. Therefore a financial plan set in motion today would still have to be flexible enough to adjust to future changes. For example, her investments would go up and down, her children might not take the path that she envisioned for them, there might be a remarriage in the future, or personal health problems could arise.

In order to meet future needs, we ran several scenarios that included likely events and their costs. These were things we could anticipate presently, such as college expenses for the kids. This is called scenario planning, and it covers life's what-ifs. It would allow us to make necessary adjustments if the unexpected took place. Although no plan can determine future events with 100 percent accuracy, a year-by-year **cash flow plan** would show Judy whether meeting her objectives would be feasible.

What Is a Cash Flow Plan?

A cash flow plan tackles the rest of your life, one year at a time. It details every single source of income you have, such as Social Security, pensions, required distributions from retirement plans, deferred compensation, rental income, and income received if you decide to return to work. Some of these income sources start in different years, and some of them end in different years, which is why a year-by-year breakdown is important. Note that some of the income sources have different tax consequences.

Such a plan would calculate mortgage and other debt payments year by year until they were paid off and would also include all of the various insurance premiums you owed. If you decided to return to work and started contributing to a retirement plan, it would factor that outflow along with the tax savings for making those retirement contributions.

The cash flow plan would also consider tax-deductible items—such as property tax and charitable contributions— separately from other types of expenses. This is because these items reduce your taxes and thus your overall expenses for each year. They also change from year to year. In addition, the plan should calculate your annual federal and state income tax liabilities. Unfortunately, individuals and even some financial advisors often overlook taxes when developing projections.

Next, all of us have so-called "lumpy" expenses, such as new cars, college expenses for kids, or expensive vacations. Finally there may be loans to family members—although I generally don't recommend this. In regard to loans, I have a riddle for you: What's the difference between a *close* relative and a *distant* one? A distant relative is someone you've loaned money to! As a general rule, it's better to consider any loan to a family member as a gift, which means that once the check is cut, it's best to forget about it and consider it a gift. If you don't want to do that, then don't make the loan.

The final page of the cash flow plan summarizes your income and various expenses, including taxes. This allows you to complete the next step, which is to determine whether there is an overall surplus or shortage. To figure this out, you need to look at the total income for each year and subtract the total expenses. If the income is greater than the expenses, you have a surplus; if the expenses exceed the income, you have a shortage. So what do you do if you're in the red? Unlike the feds, you can't just print money. Instead, you'll need to consider withdrawing from your investments, which leads to the next phase of the plan.

Sustainable Withdrawals for a Lifetime

If you withdraw too much from your investments year after year, you'll run out of money. Therefore it's important to carefully examine how much, or what percentage, of your total investment portfolio is being withdrawn every year. Your goal is to receive an amount that will sustain you for the rest of your life. If the amount is excessive, however, you'll have to reexamine your plan and consider the "Big 3": make more money, spend less, or sell assets. Then you should run a new scenario using those assumptions.

Another critical factor has to do with your investments: What type of interest or growth rates will they have? Keep in mind that no investment ever has the same interest or growth rates year after year for the rest of your life. Therefore, it's important to do the following two things: be conservative in your assumptions and factor in volatility. It's crucial to understand that the amount you plan to withdraw each year must be based in reality. You must also have a high level of confidence that you won't *run out of money before you run out of life*, and this belief must be based on a solid analysis.

Some clients begin working with me as a result of first having taken the DIY approach to creating a financial plan. Prior to their meeting with me, they may have gone as far as organizing their financial lives into spreadsheets and analyzing the data. At this point, they begin understanding the complexities of matters such as taxes and required minimum distributions from retirement plans. They then realize that it is in their best interest to seek expert advice—someone who will guide them through the financial maze using sophisticated resources and the most current legal and tax information. For example, at The Monitor Group, when we create a cash flow plan for our clients, we use the latest software—incorporating recent tax law changes—that generates a year-by-year analysis. It considers a client's financial data, his or her tax calculations, loan payments, and the future values of all investments.

Judy's Cash Flow Plan

Once I showed Judy her plan, we spent the next couple of meetings reviewing its most important aspects. When she saw the last three pages of the report, her facial expression revealed a peace that seemed to pulse through her veins. For the first time in her life, she had measureable and verifiable evidence that her future looked bright. She knew that she could maintain her current standard of living, she could pay off her mortgage, and she had a 90 percent probability of being able to cover her expenses to her ninety-fifth birthday.

The last three pages of her cash flow plan comprise the following:

- Withdrawal rate
- Retirement capital estimate
- Monte Carlo analysis

The withdrawal rate page revealed the percentage of her investment portfolio that would be withdrawn each year. As long as her withdrawal rate was below 5 percent annually, my assessment was that it would be sustainable.

The retirement capital estimate showed the value of her investment portfolio at the end of each year. It factored in each year's surpluses or shortages as well as the assumed after-tax investment return. The projection estimated that at ninety-five years of age, she would still have money left in her investment portfolio, which was certainly good news for Judy.

The static investment return assumption of her retirement capital estimate did not factor in volatility—in other words, the ups and downs of various investments. Therefore, the final page used what's called a Monte Carlo analysis. The term "Monte

Carlo" refers to the World War II code word for the probabilistic analysis scientists used to assess the potential outcomes of dropping an atomic bomb. Judy's Monte Carlo analysis ran ten thousand simulations of her financial data and varied the return each year. We took that same analytical tool and applied it to the variation in investment returns. This is called stochastic modeling. If you're interested in learning more, you can read the seminal article written by the founder of The Monitor Group, Lynn Hopewell. Titled "Decision Making Under Conditions of Uncertainty: A Wakeup Call for the Financial Planning Profession," it appeared in the October 1997 issue of the *Journal of Financial Planning*.[1]

Judy's cash flow plan enabled her to make better decisions regarding the matters that would impact her life most. At any given time, she could meet with me and ask, "What if I wanted to do _____?" We could make a few adjustments, create a new scenario, and evaluate whether what she proposed would be OK or if it would increase the probability she would be a bag lady. As a result, she could avoid making financially disastrous missteps in the future.

Because of our work together, Judy's life and her decisions about money were now grounded in reality. We didn't stop there though. Every few years, we would update the cash flow plan in order to accommodate changes in her circumstances. Think of making corrections to a cash flow plan as you would holding a car's steering wheel. Driving a car requires making constant small corrections to keep the vehicle on track. If, on the other hand, you resolutely gripped the steering wheel in one position

---

1. This article is available at http://spwfe.fpanet.org:10005/public/Unclassified%20Records/FPA%20
Journal%20April%202004%20-%20Best%20of%2025%20Years_%20Decision%20Making%20Under%20
Conditions%20of%20Uncertai.pdf

despite a bend in the road, you would most likely wind up in a ditch.

Judy was now on course. With her plan in place, she was free to focus on other important aspects of her life. She experienced peace and confidence that were rooted in data created with sophisticated financial planning software. She understood the intricacies of the cash flow plan because I provided explanations in plain English. She knew that she could pass ideas along to me, and if I believed that they would have a bad financial result, I would let her know right away. No doubt her husband's death left her both emotionally distraught and full of financial uncertainty. Through our collaboration, however, she gained newfound self-assurance, which led to a freedom to live her life the way she wanted.

In the next two chapters, we'll address another life crisis as we explore what to do when you lose your career.

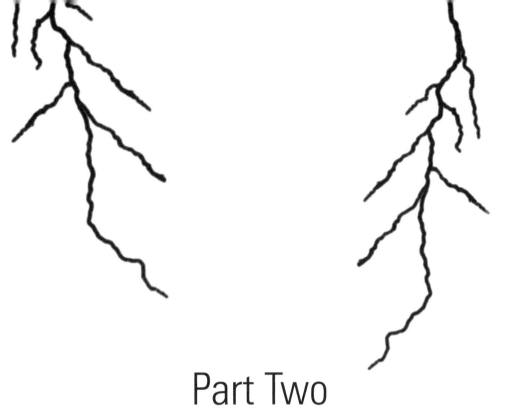

Part Two

What If I Lost My Career?

Chapter 3

Envision, then Act

It's a recession when your neighbor loses his job;
it's a depression when you lose your own.
—*Harry S. Truman*

Planning Ahead

Whenever I hear reports about bleak job prospects for recent college grads, I can certainly relate to how it feels. When I graduated from college in 1975, the nation had been hammered by a three-pronged economic assault: we were entrenched in a seemingly endless recession, the Arab oil embargo resulted in long lines at gas stations (that is, if your local filling station even had any fuel), and unemployment numbers were through the roof. I remember reading a story in *New York Magazine*'s September 1975 issue about a cab driver with a doctorate—despite his advanced degree, he couldn't find any other line of work. If all that didn't seem bad enough, the recently ended Vietnam War and the fallout from Watergate both called into question our collective trust in government. It was under these unfavorable circumstances that I earned my bachelor's degree in transportation from the University of Arkansas. Given all the possible setbacks, I felt very fortunate to get a job upon graduation.

At twenty-two years of age, I accepted a position with an oil company, Conoco (now ConocoPhillips), to work in its distribution department. A few years later, I took another step up the job ladder and joined Cities Service Company, part of which was the gas station chain Citgo. My career in transportation motivated me to study for an Interstate Commerce Commission certification. The ICC was a federal government entity that regulated transportation in the US. I passed the comprehensive exam and earned the title of ICC Practitioner–Class B, which was essentially a law degree for transportation matters. My certification was nationally recognized and would advance my career, result in a salary spike, and ensure job security . . . or so I thought.

In the early 1980s, President Jimmy Carter initiated the deregulation of transportation and began the process of eliminating the ICC. His successor, President Ronald Reagan, hammered the final nails in both coffins. Then the division of Cities Service Company that I worked for was sold off to a venture capital group. Shortly after the acquisition, I discovered my new employer was hemorrhaging red ink. In summary, federal deregulation of my industry and the demise of the ICC made my certification and specialized knowledge obsolete, and the new company I was working for was in trouble. As a result, I found myself hating going to work, and I felt trapped in a dead-end situation.

I shared my frustration with a friend, and he suggested that I read the book *What Color Is Your Parachute?* by Richard Bolles. I immediately bought it and began to work my way through it.

When I say "work," I mean it. This book isn't casual reading. To get the most out of it, you've got to put pen to paper and complete exercises that help you determine what you're good at, what you like to do, where you want to live, and much more. I wasn't the only one reading this book. It was originally self-published in 1970 and commercially published in 1972. To date, more than ten million copies have been sold worldwide. I still have the copy I purchased in 1983. Bolles's book leads to my first recommendation: if you want to make a career switch, read *What Color Is Your Parachute?* In this chapter, I'll explain why it's important to look for your new job while you're still working in your current position, and then I'll provide six steps to creating lasting and fulfilling career change.

The Pitfalls of Procrastination

I've noticed a disconcerting trend. These days, young people seem too eager to quit their jobs before they have another one lined up, and once they're unemployed, they take their sweet time looking for new work. Yes, it's a broad generalization, and I know that there are plenty of exceptions. For those who feel no urgency to find employment, however, there are clear consequences to *not* moving quickly. If you lose your job, have a high amount of debt, and have very little cash to cover expenses, then you're in serious danger of financial disaster. In fact, you've increased your probability of being forced to declare bankruptcy. You may even have to resort to imposing on friends or family for a place to sleep and eat. Postponing getting a new job will create a work gap in your résumé that may make it difficult for you to get hired because potential employers may question the long lapse between positions. Most of all, prolonged unemployment is emotionally stressful, and being desperate to find a job is no fun at all.

So why wait for the layoff notice before beginning your career search? Instead, take action while you're still earning money. In my case, after working through *What Color Is Your Parachute?* I knew that I needed to make a complete career change and begin the process of looking *while I was still working full-time.* My search led me to financial planning, which was a relatively new profession with an incredible upward trajectory. Lynn Hopewell, the founder of my current firm, The Monitor Group, once shared with me the advice that his Harvard Business School professor told him: "May you find a job in the right industry at the right time." I was fortunate to have attained that, as the financial planning profession was just beginning to take off, along with the stock market rally that began in August 1982.

The Truth about Job Security (or the Lack of It)

A 2010 study by the US Bureau of Labor Statistics found that "the average person born in the latter years of the baby boom held 11 jobs from age 18 to age 44."[2] No doubt, the days of working for forty years for one company are numbered. The reasons are many. Sometimes career switches are due to corporate downsizing, but frequently they take place because people are frustrated with their jobs and seek change.

I remember a not-so-funny get well card for a coworker that read, "Here are four words that will motivate you to get

---

2. "Number of Jobs Held, Labor Market Activity, and Earnings Growth Among the Youngest Baby Boomers: Results From a Longitudinal Survey Summary," September 2010, http://www.bls.gov/news.release/nlsoy.nr0.htm.

well soon: *You can be replaced!*" If you're convinced that you have the kind of job that will last you to retirement, think again. In a capitalistic system, a company's primary loyalty is to its shareholders, who are the owners. Business leaders may give lip service to clichés such as "Our employees come first," or "Our most important asset is people," but don't be fooled, because it's all about the stockholders. The company must make profits to stay in business, while those who have risked their capital to invest in the company (the stockholders) want to maximize profits and decrease expenses. For most businesses, the largest expense category is wages and benefits, which means that if an organization's bottom line nosedives and you aren't an owner, then *you are expendable*.

Despite these harsh capitalistic truths, the system works. You just have to understand the role you play and how to position yourself to succeed. For example, I previously owned my own business, and currently I'm part owner of The Monitor Group. I've put a significant amount of personal savings on the line investing in this business, and I want to realize a return that compensates me for that risk. Because I've played the role of employee in my previous career and shareholder in my current role, I understand that unless you're an owner, your job is at the mercy of those who run the business that you work for.

In addition, it was commonplace decades ago for companies to fire workers just before they became eligible for pension benefits—talk about dirty tricks! This practice has become less common due to anti-age-discrimination laws and the Employee Retirement Income Security Act (ERISA) of 1974, which regulates company retirement plans—but it still happens. It's tempting for companies to replace highly paid folks in their fifties and sixties with young people who command lower salaries.

"It's for these reasons that I avoided the cutthroat world of corporate America and opted to become a public servant instead," you may say. After all, law enforcement and public safety professionals, teachers, and government employees may not always earn the best salaries, but the trade-off for lower wages is a solid pension and job security—or so people think. But even these jobs are expendable. An employee's so-called permanent or tenured status can quickly be replaced with a pink slip when the government can't pay the bills. The bottom line is that whatever your job situation, you can't bury your head in the sand and think that your employer will always take care of you.

The Six-Step Career Makeover

You now realize that lifelong employment at your present company is tenuous at best, delusional at worst. You also recognize that there are better opportunities waiting for you. The following are six steps designed to create lasting and fulfilling career change:

1. Envision your dream job, and then act on it.
2. Consider self-employment.
3. Consider a career in sales.
4. Obtain essential education and training.
5. Develop networking skills.
6. Create a cash reserve and get out of debt.

Envision Your Dream Job, and Then Act on It

What Color is Your Parachute? will guide you through a process of determining your ideal career. Once you've completed this step, you'll need to conduct "informational interviews" with people who may be able to assist you in making your goal a reality. An informational interview is very different from a job interview. It's more akin to networking because you're asking people in related fields to assist and give you ideas and feedback. You'll be pleasantly surprised by how the simple question, "Can you help me figure out my future?" will be greeted with helpful assistance.

Consider Self-Employment

If you're looking for job security and financial success, I encourage you to consider starting your own business. While working independently may seem like a risky proposition, I'm convinced that the highest degree of job security is available to those who own their own companies. Why? Because business owners have much more control than their employees. After all, their customers are the only ones who can fire them.

You may have heard discouraging statistics that claim that 90 percent of small businesses fail. There is research, however, that counters this high-failure-rate figure. A Small Business Administration study, for example, found that 70 percent of small businesses survive for two years and roughly half for five years.[3] Furthermore, the National Federation of Independent Business conducted a study in conjunction with Wells Fargo Bank and found a similar five-year survival rate. The NFIB estimated that over the lifetime of a business, 39 percent were profitable, 30 percent broke even, and the rest either lost money or fell into the category of "undetermined." [4]

If you're going to start your own business, be very analytical and develop a written plan. Carefully calculate your anticipated

---

3. Mark Henricks, "Why the Small Business Failure Rate is 90 Percent Smoke and Mirrors," September 2, 2010, www.bnet.com.
4. Karen Klein, "What's Behind the High Small-Biz Failure Rates?" Business Week, September 30, 1999.

expenses—and then double them. Determine your projected revenue—and then cut it in half. This is because things rarely go as expected with a new business; costs are usually higher than anticipated and revenue is often less than expected.

Consider a Career in Sales

My father once told me that if you're a good salesperson, you'll always have a job. He wasn't even in sales—he was a corporate attorney—but my dad came to this conclusion after decades of observing others in the working world. Commission-based sales is a career that may seem very risky. I'll be the first to acknowledge that success in sales is tough because you're compensated only for the amount of deals you close, so a dip in performance will directly affect your earnings. However, the law of supply and demand will work in your favor if you have the natural gifts or the desire to learn how to become an effective salesperson, and you're willing to work very hard.

Neither self-employment nor sales is easy. If you've got the "right stuff," however, you can find these careers immensely rewarding, both emotionally and financially. In my case, I went from being an employee in a large corporation to taking a sales position in financial services. Then I became self-employed. The transitions from one role to another were extremely difficult. I experienced a long, steep learning curve to gain and master sales and self-employment skills. The hard work paid off, however. As Confucius said, "Do something you love and you'll never work a day in your life." While that's a bit misleading—self-employment is very hard work—the truth is that the investment of time and money can be immensely rewarding if you're engaged in a business that you truly enjoy.

Obtain Essential Education and Training

In the late seventies, factories throughout the northeast and upper midwest regions of the United States were closing their doors. The result was massive unemployment. These economically depressed regions eventually were referred to as the Rust Belt. Sadly many of the Rust Belt factories never reopened. The situation was so tragic and widespread that singer Billy Joel recorded a song titled "Allentown" that captured the hardships that millions of former industrial workers endured. The unemployed individuals ended up following two broad paths:

- One group went on welfare and continued living off the tax revenues of productive American workers.
- The other group enrolled in educational and training programs that prepared them for different careers.

The demise of industries that comprised the Rust Belt points to the harsh reality that everyone in this country must acknowledge: with jaw-dropping speed, new technologies make obsolete what was once the latest and greatest. One just needs to look at the evolution of the Dow Jones Industrial Average for proof. The Dow, a widely quoted stock market index, contains thirty companies. Charles Dow established it in 1896 with twelve companies. More than one hundred years later, there is only one company from the original list still in the Dow— General Electric. All the others went bankrupt, were broken up by the government, or were merged into other companies. Consider how word processors put typewriter manufacturers out of business, Napster and iTunes forever altered the recording industry, and the automobile destroyed buggy whip makers. On the other hand, constant change also creates new opportunities for those who are open to what the future holds.

I remember a television program that interviewed those who had formerly worked in steel mills and other factories in the Rust Belt. These folks had gone back to school or received training in entirely new careers. Through hard work and adjusting to change, they found jobs in software and other high-tech industries. Not only were they making more money than they had in their former jobs, but also their working conditions were vastly improved. Gone were the dirty and dangerous factories and mines where they had clocked in every day. The television documentary pointed out that these workers didn't get their new jobs by sitting at home, watching TV, and waiting for someone to come knocking on their doors. Instead, they recognized the challenge and the potential opportunity that would only be possible through education and training.

Just as some kind of educational degree is necessary for most adults to get their first so-called grown-up job, additional education will most likely be necessary if you're making a career switch. When you take care of this while you're still at your current job, you've got the cash flow to cover retraining expenses. Once you've completed the necessary coursework, training, or both, you're ready to move into a new field right away. This points to the importance of being proactive. There is no downside to being more educated. Yes, it may cost money—in some cases lots of it. I got a master's degree in taxation at the age of fifty-four, and it was expensive. Obtaining any degree is an investment in your future earning power, which means that the payoff can be huge. Will it guarantee you a high-paying job that you'll love? No. It substantially improves the odds, though. You'll be a much stronger candidate for whatever job you seek because you'll rise to the top of the hiring list. Remember, when you're competing for a job, coming in second usually means that you won't get hired.

Develop Networking Skills

You've probably heard the saying, "It's not what you know, it's who you know." Actually, I think it's both. It is what you know (education and credentials) *and* who you know (personal and professional connections). Meeting and getting to know as many people as you can are essential steps to advancing your career. Those who aren't particularly sociable often shudder at the thought of schmoozing and reaching out, but networking can fit nearly any personality type. If you're an introvert, it helps if you join an organization where you'll meet like-minded individuals. That way you'll increase the chances of creating an immediate connection.

In addition, consider joining community, civic, and faith-based organizations that align with your interests. Your networking community can potentially help you in ways that you can't even imagine. Don't just join and attend meetings; get involved in committees and volunteer to take on leadership positions. This points to one important characteristic of a successful networker: *always give first.* When your priority is to contribute your time and talents for the good of the organization itself, the rewards will come naturally.

Create a Cash Reserve and Get Out of Debt

In 234 BC, the Roman statesman Cato the Elder said, "Cessation of work is not accompanied by cessation of expenses." In addition to the psychological and educational preparation required for career change, there are two critical financial planning measures to take care of as well.

First, you must create a cash reserve, which is also called an emergency fund. Career switch or not, every working person should have one. The emergency fund should cover a minimum of three months of your living expenses. In order to determine a cash reserve amount, you need to figure out your monthly living expenses. Your emergency fund should be invested in something safe and liquid. In other words, it should be in a place where you can access the cash quickly and without penalty or delay. I recommend that my clients place theirs in bank savings accounts or money market funds. No, they won't earn a high interest rate, but that's not the objective. In the event that my clients experience job loss, they can withdraw money right away to pay living expenses. A six-month emergency fund would give you even more leeway to find a new position—all the better if you can do this.

Second, get out of debt. Dave Ramsey's excellent book *Total Money Makeover* provides readers a great strategy for eliminating debt and building an emergency fund. You may think that slashing debt should come *before* saving for a rainy day. Instead, Ramsey suggests that you first put $1,000 into an emergency fund. Only then should you begin paying off your debts, except your mortgage. I agree with his approach because it ensures that you have something in reserve ($1,000 minimum) while implementing a debt reduction plan *right away*.

To do away with debt, you first list all of your liabilities—with the exceptions of your home mortgage and home equity line of credit. Then you place your debts in order from smallest to largest. Examples include car and personal loans and outstanding credit card balances. Next to each item, determine the minimum payment and the interest rate. The following is an example:

Loan	Amt Owed	Minimum Payment	Months To Pay	Interest Rate
MasterCard	1,000	25.00	61	18%
Visa	2,000	50.00	78	24%
Car Loan	15,000	375.00	44	5%
Total	18,000	450.00		

Notice that the total monthly debt amount is $450. At this point, you start each month by tackling the smallest debt first, while making the minimum payment on all the other debts. Using the example I provided, you'd start with the MasterCard. Let's say that you decided to increase your total debt payment to $600 instead of your current $450, which is $150 more per month. Add that $150 to the $25 monthly MasterCard payment. In other words, you're now paying $175 per month toward the credit card balance. Following this formula, this item would be free and clear in just seven months. Once the MasterCard is paid off, take the $175 per month you were paying for it and apply it to the $50 Visa payment, so the total monthly Visa payment will now be $225. At this monthly amount, within nine months you'd pay off the Visa. Once the Visa balance is zero, apply that $225 to the car loan, which will mean that your monthly car payment is now $600 per month. The good news is, instead of waiting four years, the car will be paid off in twenty-three months. Ramsey refers to this as the "debt snowball" because you pay more and more against each successive liability. As a result, your debts get paid off remarkably quickly. In most cases, it's an eighteen-month to two-year process.

Once all debts are gone, then you take that snowball amount and start building up your emergency fund. Read *Total Money Makeover* for more details. Ramsey not only provides solid advice but also adds real-world stories that illustrate the power of his money management system. The best part is that Ramsey's tools are straightforward and free of financial jargon. The bottom line is to do whatever it takes to plug the hole that's hemorrhaging your savings. If you need to get a second job delivering pizzas to generate extra cash, so be it.

How to Avoid Career Change Panic

Remember this formula: debt + joblessness = pressure. The opposite is true as well. If your overhead (monthly expenses and liabilities) is low and your cash position (assets including an emergency fund) is high, you'll be in much better shape to weather a job search that may take months. If you're laid off, you may be fortunate enough to receive a severance package that will help you stay afloat despite a prolonged period of unemployment. Do not be complacent during that severance pay period. Attack the new job hunt with vigor instead so you don't have to tap into your emergency fund or amass more debt than you may already have.

Planning ahead for a job loss will help you avoid financial ruin, maintain dignity, and remain solvent during a period of career transition. As a result, you'll be equipped to dive into your job search with confidence and peace of mind.

In the next chapter, I'll address what to do when unemployment is your current reality.

Chapter 4

Surviving Unemployment

The trouble with unemployment is that the minute you wake up in the morning you're on the job.
—comedian Slappy White

You've been handed the dreaded pink slip. In other words, you've been laid off, fired, terminated, let go, canned, or "RIF'd" (Reduction in Force)—whatever you call it, it's some of the worst information you'll ever receive. I'm sure that the pain associated with such news explains why bosses and owners have creatively crafted so many ways to basically say, "I'm sorry, your services aren't needed here anymore." So what do you do now?

Unfortunately there's no easy, one-size-fits-all salve that you can apply to your unemployed state. There are, however, basic principles that will speed up your job search and improve your prospects of getting hired. In this chapter, I'll provide six insights and one important piece of financial advice that will guide you through this financially and emotionally difficult time.

Principle 1: Avoid Résumé Red Flags

Through my experience of being a business owner, I've hired and fired many people. Between my executive assistant and me, we've seen countless job applications. Whenever we're hiring at The Monitor Group, my assistant is the first person to review all résumés. She then keeps the ones that she deems worth my review and tosses out the rest. Even after this initial screening process, the résumés that make it to my desk are often poorly written, don't reflect any relevant experience for the job the person is applying for, have large gaps in employment history, or reflect any combination of the three. In addition, another "don't hire me" warning sign is a résumé that indicates the applicant is a job-hopper. In other words, he or she has changed employers every year or two. On rare occasions, there can be a reasonable and acceptable explanation for too many jobs in too few years, but based on my experience with hiring employees, most of the time it's due to a character flaw in the individual.

Principle 2: Finding a Job Is Your New Full-Time Job

Throughout your employment, you showed up at the office, Monday through Friday, for at least eight hours a day—maybe you even worked weekends. Now that you've been laid off, you must commit the same amount of time looking for a job as you did to performing your previous job. You may wonder how you'll ever fill forty hours a week. I'll start with what you *shouldn't* do:

- Watch TV.
- Browse the Internet for fun.
- Play on your gaming console.

- Socialize with friends either online or in person—this is fake networking, so don't fool yourself.
- Take care of chores, such as cleaning the house, shopping, and cooking.

This is not to say that you cut these activities out of your life entirely. When you were gainfully employed, you participated in these activities *after your workday*; you should apply the same stringent standards to your current job search. Here's how you *should* invest your time. First, start by developing a plan and executing it. In the first chapter of *What Color is Your Parachute?*—the career guide that I introduced in the previous chapter—the author gives sixteen different job-hunting methods. Of these, he provides the "five worst ways to look for a job" and the "five best ways to look for a job."[5] Don't you think it would be important to know this? Buy the book and get to work designing your plan.

Principle 3: Be Visible; Don't Isolate Yourself

The first thing you may want to do after being laid off is to crawl under the covers and wallow. Unemployment can certainly lead to depression, which makes the job search even harder. It's a vicious cycle that can last months and lead to financial ruin. For these reasons, unemployment is the worst possible time to become a recluse. Instead, get out there and engage with your network, even if it's the very last thing you want to do. As a result, you'll be energized, and you will experience positive results.

Start by picking up the phone and contacting your colleagues and business associates. Join trade groups—and if you presently belong to one, be sure to maintain your membership and continue

5. Richard N. Bolles, *What Color is Your Parachute?* (New York: Ten Speed Press, 2007), 7–15.

to attend meetings. Keep in mind that your network also includes friends, family members, former coworkers, and past professors. Furthermore, if you experienced any level of career success, you have most likely impressed those around you. Contact these individuals. Ask if they know of people and organizations that can provide you support and guidance. Even if you didn't network while you were employed, opportunity still awaits you. There's nothing stopping you from joining organizations and contributing your time and energy starting today.

If you have sufficient cash reserves, contact people who are working in careers you are interested in and invite them to lunch and offer to pay. While the other person may insist on picking up the tab, you should still be prepared and willing to treat them to the meal. Use the one hour of one-on-one time effectively by preparing questions ahead of time and taking notes.

Take advantage of social networking as well. This doesn't include posting a Twitter update that describes what you ate for lunch. Instead use Twitter, Facebook, and LinkedIn to reach out to people who can support you in your search.

Principle 4: It's a Numbers Game

In the world of sales training, you'll often hear the phrase, "What gets measured gets done." Top sales professionals keep track of how many phone calls they've made, how many appointments they've scheduled, the number of face-to-face (or Skype-to-Skype) meetings they've had, and how many deals they've closed. Highly motivated salespeople can at any given time tell you their average commission per sale. The bottom line is that by measuring their workflow they know how many "No"s it takes to get a "Yes."

In addition, all salespeople are taught that if you don't ask, the answer is "No." On the other hand, if you do ask, the worst result possible is "No." So remember, by taking a bold step forward—asking for help, a referral, or a position within a company—you've got nothing to lose and everything to gain. Can it be embarrassing or even humiliating? Perhaps. That leads us to the next principle.

Principle 5: Be Persistent

If you don't persist during your job hunt, the result will be persistent unemployment. Calvin Coolidge, the thirtieth president of the United States, eloquently extolled the importance of persistence. I've always been a big fan of his (which might have something to do with the fact that I'm named after him). He said:

> *Nothing in the world can take the place of persistence. Talent will not; nothing in the world is more common than unsuccessful men with talent. Genius will not; unrewarded genius is almost a proverb. Education will not; the world is full of educated derelicts. Persistence and determination alone are omnipotent.*

Winston Churchill, the prime minister of England who made his mark on world history as a result of his role during the dark days of World War II, said (and I paraphrase):

> *Never, never, never give up.*

Vince Lombardi, the coach of the Green Bay Packers and later the Washington Redskins, said:

It's not whether you get knocked down; it's whether you get up.

Finally, master motivator and author Dale Carnegie said:

Most of the important things in the world have been accomplished by people who have kept on trying when there seemed to be no hope at all.

I've highlighted these quotes from notable individuals not only to inspire you, but also to encourage you to surround yourself with positive people and resources. One action that will quickly lift a troubled mood is to read the biographies of successful businesspeople. I particularly enjoyed the stories of Colonel Sanders, the founder of Kentucky Fried Chicken; Sam Walton, who started Walmart; Ray Kroc, the man behind the success of McDonald's; and Truett Cathy, who created Chick-fil-A. Studying the lives of great entrepreneurs will motivate you, and their stories will also provide you with effective business-building ideas. In nearly every instance, you'll see that they faced tremendous obstacles and often experienced heartbreaking failure before accomplishing their goals.

Looking for a job is never easy. In fact, it can be horribly discouraging. I've had friends who had been out of work for more than a year—and their unemployment had nothing to with laziness or incompetence. Despite setback after setback, they kept at their search. They continued sending out résumés and e-mails, and they enlisted the help of friends. They were always precise in their pursuit, asking others if they knew someone at a particular company or in a specific industry or field. Their hard work often resulted in jobs that were even better than their previous positions.

Principle 6: Be a Lifelong Learner

There are innumerable resources related to finding a job. The good news is that lots of them are free. Examples include podcasts, video casts, chat forums, Twitter feeds, white papers, and articles. Whether it's a book or a blog, take advantage of what's out there. Remember, however, the line between entertainment and education can sometimes become hazy, so make sure that your career research isn't really recreation.

In addition to *What Color is Your Parachute?* another powerful book is *Sweaty Palms: The Neglected Art of Being Interviewed* by H. Anthony Medley. This book gives practical and important tips on both what to do *and* what not to do before and during any interview. Don't stop reading once you land a job. Remember that in this highly competitive Information Age, there's always going to be someone—perhaps in another part of the world—who is vying for your position. Therefore, researching voraciously throughout your working years is an essential part of staying on top of your profession, maintaining a competitive edge, and being able to quickly adapt to change.

When to Get a Job While Searching for a Job

Sometimes you'll need to seek temporary work while you're still looking for a job. This may be because you've run out of your emergency fund or you didn't have one at all. In order to find a short-term job, you may need to work through a temporary employment agency. They may assign you a position that you feel is beneath you. For example, you may have been a well-paid engineer and now you're answering phones at a front desk. Although the experience may be humbling, one benefit of temporary work is that you'll avoid gaps in your work history. You're also out in the working world and meeting new people.

As I pointed out earlier, future employers aren't impressed by long lapses between jobs. During an interview for a potential position, you can explain the reasons behind your temporary work. The interviewer may view your honesty as a positive because it displays good character, as opposed to laziness, sloth, or lack of motivation. Always remember to practice caution when using an employment agency. For instance, never pay an agency a fee to find work for you. Rather the company that uses the agency to hire employees should cover all fees.

Financial Advice: Roll Over Your 401(k)

Many people who leave an employer—regardless of the reason behind their departure—make a huge mistake: they keep their 401(k) (or any other qualified retirement plan covered by the Employee Retirement Income Security Act) parked at their previous employer. Why do they do this? The reasons range from uncertainty as to what they're supposed to do to just plain laziness. In other words, there really are no good explanations. By keeping your 401(k) plan with your previous employer, you'll experience the following disadvantages that are inherent in *all* 401(k)s:

- Limited **investment choices**
- High costs
- Potential overexposure to company stock
- Potential failure to pay attention to the performance of your investments and neglect of the overall management of your **portfolio**

- Unnecessary red tape (For example, you may have to contact the HR department of your previous employer if you want to withdraw funds or make changes to your account.)

One advantage to having an ERISA plan used to be that it provided liability protection in the event that you were sued or went bankrupt. That was changed as a result of the Bankruptcy Abuse Prevention and Consumer Protection Act of 2005 and a separate Supreme Court decision in 2005. Therefore, that sole benefit of ERISA plans no longer exists for terminated employees. IRAs (Individual Retirement Accounts) now offer virtually the same safeguards as retirement plans that qualify under ERISA regulations. The Bankruptcy Abuse Prevention and Consumer Protection Act protects up to $1 million in IRA assets in the event of bankruptcy. In other types of lawsuits, creditor protection of IRAs can vary from state to state. Keep in mind that you can purchase umbrella liability insurance for very little money (about $200 a year for $1 million of coverage). This would preserve all of your assets, including IRAs, from creditors, and this is my preferred strategy.

For all these reasons, I strongly recommend that you roll over the retirement plan from your former company into your own self-directed IRA. With that said, there is a tax "gotcha" you must be aware of: you must carefully fill out the paperwork and indicate that you want a "direct rollover." Any other option you select may result in significant taxes and penalties or an irrevocable lifetime annuity. Another "gotcha" has to do with 401(k) loans. If you leave your employer for any reason and have an outstanding loan amount, that loan balance immediately becomes a taxable distribution—you'll owe income taxes plus, if you're under age fifty-nine-and-a-half, a 10 percent tax penalty—and there is no way around it. For this reason, I highly discourage 401(k) loans in all but the most dire circumstances.

Pay off the loan with other funds, if possible, if you see a job change coming. If you don't know what to do or how to fill out this form, my advice is to seek the assistance of a competent CFP® Professional who has taken care of many direct rollovers. One last word regarding your retirement plan: if your period of unemployment is stretching your finances thin, consider tapping into your IRA only as a *last resort*. Unfortunately every dollar you withdraw from an IRA will be taxable, although there is an exception to the pre-fifty-nine-and-a-half penalty if you use the IRA money to pay health insurance premiums while unemployed.

The harsh consequences of unemployment can easily suck the life out of your finances and self-esteem. By following the principles in this chapter, I can't guarantee that you'll find your dream job right away. What I can state with complete confidence, however, is that if you adhere to the advice that I've outlined, then you're ahead of the vast majority who are competing against you for the same position. Therefore, don't take my tips as mere suggestions from which you can pick and choose. These are universal job search truths that come from years of learning from my own setbacks as well as my career successes and my experience in hiring and firing employees. Ingrain these career essentials in your mind, and put them into practice right away. In other words, be a "doer" and not just a reader.

In the next chapter, we'll deal with losses associated with investments.

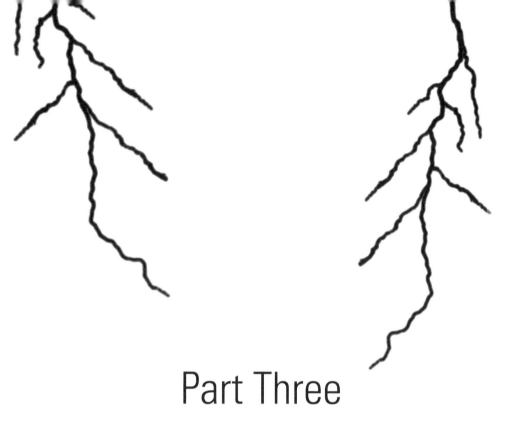

Part Three

What If I Lost My Investments?

Chapter 5

Looking Forward

Don't gamble. Take all your savings and
buy a good stock, and hold it 'til it goes up, then sell it.
If it don't go up, don't buy it.
— Will Rogers

In Tom Brokaw's *New York Times* best seller, *The Greatest Generation*, the journalist and author highlighted the accomplishments of my parents' generation. These individuals won World War II and were the driving force behind America's ascendancy as a world leader.

Along with their exceptional achievements, the Greatest Generation also survived the hardships of the Great Depression. They experienced the aftermath of the 1929 stock market crash and the subsequent failure of the banking system, both of which led to massive unemployment. The unprecedented economic slump wreaked havoc on countless people, resulting in an entire generation of individuals who lost trust in and remained skeptical of financial institutions for far longer than the Great Depression itself. As a result, many adults spent the rest of their lives keeping their savings in their mattresses instead of in banks and the stock market. One exception was US savings bonds. A significant number of people ended up investing in these low-yielding bonds, but this was often more an act of patriotism than investment acumen.

In recent history, the US stock markets suffered two major declines. The first was from March 2000 to February 2003, and the second was from October 2007 to March 2009. During the first period, the technology stock bubble burst and on September 11, 2001, we experienced the terrorist bombings of the World Trade Center and the Pentagon. In the second decline, the real estate market peaked and then plummeted and banks failed. Many individuals with more than $100,000[6] in any one account at a failed bank saw their savings over the $100,000 limit disappear. In addition, in 2008 the stock market tanked, and the result of all this was the highest unemployment rate since the recession in 1982.

More than seventy years after the 1929 crash, the events that took place from 2000 to 2009 have resulted in what I fear is a new group of doubt-filled people. These individuals may hold the same contempt for financial institutions as those who survived the Great Depression. Clients and friends have already told me that they'll never again put their hard-earned money in the stock market. I'm continually astonished when I hear that both individual and institutional investors are keeping their money in very low-yielding US Treasury bills, money market funds, and bank accounts, which is to say that they are willing to earn virtually no interest on their money as long as they have a guarantee of safety.[7] Unfortunately such fear-based investing

---

6. This was the maximum FDIC insured amount at the time.
7. In 2008, the FDIC raised the insured amount for bank accounts to $250,000. The Dodd-Frank Wall Street Reform and Consumer Protection Act, signed into law on July 21, 2010, made this $250,000 FDIC coverage limit permanent.

may have disastrous results, as I'll point out later. In this chapter, I'll help dispel investing misgivings, and I'll provide a solid foundation from which to approach your **portfolio**.

All I Hear Is Doom and Gloom about the US Economy. Why Bother?

In an article in *MarketWatch,* a subsidiary of Dow Jones & Company, Mark Hulbert contrasted mainstream press coverage of the recession of 2008–2009 with that of news signaling that the US GDP had reached prerecession numbers.[8] The recession was bad news and the increase in US GDP was good news.

"You'd think that the complete recovery from the worst economic downturn since the Great Depression would be big news. But you'd be wrong," Hulbert wrote. According to the article, one of the reasons behind the lack of press coverage of positive financial news is the media's emphasis on fear-based reporting. So much for objective journalism.

It's easy to get caught up in the twenty-four-hour media cycle with its constant barrage of bad news that could sour even the most positive mood. Despite what news reports say, I am unabashedly optimistic about our country's long-term economic prospects. Far from rose-colored glasses, my observation is a result of the following four distinctly American qualities:

- Risk-taking
- Creativity
- Innovation
- Entrepreneurship

8. Mark Hulbert, "We Shall Overcome," *MarketWatch*, December 24, 2010.

As long as these four factors form the fibers of our nation's economic fabric, new companies with great ideas will continue to emerge, and from both the point of view of our investment portfolios and the US economy as a whole, we'll all benefit. On the other hand, when businesses no longer want to make a profit . . . that's when it's time to sell all your investments and move to another country. Frankly I cannot foresee that happening during our lifetime and the lifetimes of our children.

Taking a historical perspective, the following is a very short list of innovations that weren't around when I graduated from college in 1975. Seemingly overnight, these once nonexistent products have become absolute necessities:

- Personal computers, laptops, and tablets such as iPads
- The Internet
- Cell phones and smartphones such as the BlackBerry, Droid, and iPhone
- MP3 players and iPods
- Hybrid cars

A Very Brief History of Modern Investing

The Greatest Generation endured tremendous hardship and sacrifice. They also were the benefactors of two major financial innovations that comprised two legs of the "three-legged stool of retirement," which is a term I learned when I entered this profession in the mid-1980s. Social Security was part of Franklin Delano Roosevelt's New Deal, and pension plans came about around the same time. In addition to these two new deals (pun intended), the stool's third leg is personal savings, which included investments.

Today pension plans are pretty much a thing of the past, unless you work for the federal or state government or a few very large corporations. Most other corporations have terminated pensions and replaced them with 401(k) savings plans, while smaller companies never had them in the first place.

As far as Social Security is concerned, it's still a fact of life. According to one study, however, many people in their twenties and thirties believe that it's more likely they'll encounter an alien from outer space than receive Social Security benefits when they retire.[9]

So if you don't have a pension and won't hold your breath for Social Security benefits, that leaves you with a one-legged stool. That is, all you can count on for retirement income will be your own personal savings and retirement accounts. A one-legged stool is quite unstable, unless that leg is substantial.

So in what will you place your retirement savings? There are a plethora of businesses and investment vehicles clamoring for your savings and retirement money. The following is a short, and far from complete, list:

- Bank savings accounts
- *CDs* (Certificates of Deposit)
- Bonds (US savings bonds, municipal bonds, corporate bonds, government bonds, and foreign bonds)
- Annuities (fixed and variable rate, and immediate and deferred)
- Real estate

> CDs are a safe, low-interest-rate savings account offered only by a US bank, usually with some period of time (one year, two years, five years, etc.) associated with it. If cashed out early, there is normally an early withdrawal penalty. CDs are insured by the US government up to $250,000 per account.

9. 60 Plus Association, "Close Encounters of the Social Security Kind," August 17, 1999, http://60plus.org/aw196/.

- **Mutual funds,** of which there are nearly countless types and varieties
- Individual stocks
- ETFs (Exchange Traded Funds)
- Oil and gas
- Gold and other commodities
- Limited partnerships
- Notes (real estate and business loans)
- Business interests (investing in a friend's or neighbor's startup company)
- IRAs (Individual Retirement Accounts) and Roth IRAs
- 401(k)s, 403(b)s, SEP-IRAs, SIMPLE plans, 457 plans, 401(a) Profit Sharing plans, Thrift Savings Plans, and other employer-provided retirement plans regulated by ERISA
- 529 Plans and Education (Coverdell) Savings Accounts for college

This is just a partial list. Given the numerous types, how are you expected to master all the combinations and permutations of these investment products, let alone the tax implications that go along with them? You essentially have two choices:

1. DIY (do-it-yourself)
2. Hire a trusted advisor

DIY Requires TIME

When the Internet became the world's most powerful resource of information, suddenly everyone could become an investor. Transaction costs plummeted to $10 per trade or less, and stock research charts became free. The stockbroker's career seemed doomed. After all, who needed one when you could do your own research and trade online? According to a study by DALBAR, Inc., a leading financial services marketing firm, and published by J.P. Morgan, over a twenty-year period ending December 31, 2009, the following was the annual *average rate of return* for the following investments:

S&P 500 stock index	8.2%
Bonds	7.0%
Oil	6.7%
Gold	5.2%
International stocks	4.4%
Homes	3.2%
Average Investor	***2.3%***

What makes the final figure even more shocking is that inflation averaged *2.8 percent per year* over the same twenty years. So why did Joe-the-Average-Investor perform so poorly with his portfolio not even beating inflation? The answer is simple: *he bought and sold at the wrong time.* Although what he invested in was fine, he made poor decisions that were driven by his emotions. This points to the fact that faster access to information and more of it does not make anyone a better investor.

Despite the dismal results of the average investor, DIY investing is a valid option for many people. In order to separate the DIY wannabe from the real deal, I coined the acronym TIME. It will help you determine whether you're ready to take on the formidable task of do-it-yourself investing.

T: Time. Are you someone with a demanding job and a spouse and kids? Are you retired with a schedule full of activities and recreational pursuits? If so, you must understand that investing requires an immense commitment of time for research, trading, and making buy and sell decisions.

I: Interest. Does the thought of new investment opportunities and future economic trends make you want to hop online and read the *Wall Street Journal,* pick up a copy of *Smart Money,* or tune in to CNBC? In that case, investing on your own may be a worthwhile endeavor. Such individuals are a rare breed, and I can spot them right away. They're investment news junkies, who ask lots of highly technical questions and can't seem to ever research and learn enough. On the other hand, if figuring out the intricacies of investments and tax codes bores or even scares you, you're probably better off working with an expert.

M: Millions. Do you have a large amount of money to invest due to your personal savings, retirement account, or perhaps a significant inheritance? Many people feel fine investing relatively small amounts ($10,000 to $250,000) on their own. But when it comes to their $2 million 401(k) rollover, an inheritance worth millions, or a $1 million (or more) **life insurance** death benefit, their comfort level plunges. The seemingly instantaneous appearance of large amounts of money—starting at $1 million from what I've seen—immediately fills a person with uncertainty. Fears such as "I don't want to make a mistake and lose my nest egg" or "I'll never have another opportunity to have this amount of money and I don't want to blow it" quickly surface. A recently retired airline pilot told me, "To get a check for seven figures and not know what to do is really scary!"

Even if a DIY investor is successful, he must consider what would happen when he dies. For instance, if he is married, what if his surviving spouse has no interest in managing the portfolio?

In this case, the do-it-yourself approach impacts not only the investor himself but also his wife, children, and other close family members.

E: Emotions. There's an old refrain in the investment community: Bulls make money, bears make money, but pigs get slaughtered. Most investments do fairly well over time. The problem is that most people succumb to the powerful emotions of fear, greed, or both. This explains why the average investor in the study I described earlier only earned 2.3 percent over a twenty-year period. They tinker with their investments and end up buying and selling at the wrong times. When the stock market is up, they feel confident, which means that they buy when prices are high. When the stock market nosedives, they become very fearful, and as a consequence they sell when prices are low. They fall prey to the following basic investing principle:

Buy high + sell low = lose money

Six Types of Risk That Are Often Overlooked

When it comes to investing, most people don't understand risk. They think that it only refers to a loss of principal in the short-term. They don't realize that there are many types of risk. I'll highlight six of them.

Interest Rate Risk

Interest rate risk is peculiar to bonds, and it can be very confusing. There's an inverse relationship between interest rate changes and the price of bonds: if interest rates go up, the value of the bond you own goes down; if interest rates decrease, the value of your bond increases. However, if you hold onto your bond until it matures, you'll receive the full price of the bond—as long as it doesn't default.

Default Risk

Default risk also applies to bonds. If you own a corporation's bond issues and that corporation files for Chapter 11 bankruptcy protection (as many well-known companies did during the decade of 2001–2009[10]), you could lose your entire investment in that corporate bond.

Bondholders, however, do stand ahead of other investors when they're waiting in the creditor line, and they may receive some value for their bonds, depending on the bankruptcy court's decision. Bonds issued by the US government are considered to be some of the world's safest investments. After all, if the US defaults, then we're all in trouble! There are also bonds issued by state and local governments, which are called municipal bonds. These do have some default risk. For example, in 1994, Orange County, California, famously defaulted on its municipal bonds. In late 2010 and into 2011, there was great concern that many state and local governments would default on their municipal bond issues. The bottom line is that different types of bonds have different levels of default risk.

Inflation Risk

Inflation risk is associated with long life, which is usually a good thing. If you live too long, however, and the increase in your cost of living exceeds your investment return, you may eventually not have enough money to support yourself. For example, imagine

---

10. These included Pacific Gas & Electric, Enron, Global Crossing, Adelphia Communications, WorldCom, Tyco International, US Airways, Conseco, Trump Entertainment Resorts, Delta Airlines, Northwest Airlines, Delphi, IndyMac Bancorp, Lehman Brothers, Washington Mutual, Tribune Group, General Growth Properties, Chrysler, and General Motors.

an individual who refuses to invest in the stock market. Perhaps he followed a bad stock tip in the past and never wants to get burned again. As a result, he vows to only put his money in safe investments, such as US Treasury bills that earn 2 percent interest. If inflation averages 3.5 percent over the rest of his life, his so-called *safe investment* will result in him safely going broke. In other words, while his principal is protected from a short-term decline in value, the withdrawals he must make during his retirement will increase each year, which will eventually cause him to go broke.

Business Risk

If you invest your money in any one business, even one you start yourself, you run the risk of the company going out of business. This is especially true for employees of very large corporations who have a significant part of their retirement plan money and other money invested in their employer's stock. The 2005 Enron collapse is a horrific example of this. Enron employees who were heavily invested in Enron stock lost all (or most) of their nest egg (see prior footnote under "Default Risk").

Diversifiable Risk

Academics call diversifiable risk nonsystematic risk. You can completely eliminate business risk (referred to as systematic risk) by simply diversifying. It's possible to construct a low-cost investment portfolio that contains small amounts of more than twelve thousand separate companies, thereby greatly reducing risk.

Market Risk

Market risk is risk associated with the volatility of the stock market. While market dips make headline news—and sometimes these can be significant—over time (five years or more) they're not as great as most people think. In fact, this risk can be reduced by simply not investing all of your money in the stock market.

How to Develop Your Portfolio

The first question you should ask yourself is, "What proportion of my portfolio should be in cash equivalents such as bonds, Treasury bills, bank savings accounts, and money market funds, and what proportion should be in stocks, real estate, or other equity investments?"

"But, Cal, the stock market's ups and downs make my stomach turn. Can't I just avoid investing in equities?" clients will often ask me. First I share with them the concept of safely going broke, as I explained earlier. Then I point out that the stock market's movements are overblown in the media because they're an easy way for news outlets to create headlines.

Contrast the media frenzy over the stock market's activity with that of real estate. People who own houses and income properties don't check the newspaper or their iPhones every hour to see if their property values have gone up or down. In fact, most don't check on a weekly, monthly, or even yearly basis. If they did, they'd probably react the same way that many investors do regarding the stock market.

Although this will never make front page news, the fact of the matter is that given enough time, market risk is never permanent, unless an investor sells when prices are down. What's key is to always consider long-term performance rather than hourly, daily, weekly, and monthly market fluctuations.

Few People Can Accurately Assess Risk on Their Own

When I visited with my ophthalmologist, he told me his daughter needed eye surgery. "Will you perform the procedure yourself?" I asked.

"Absolutely not!" he answered. The doctor explained that physicians virtually never operate on their own family members because emotions could cloud their judgment and affect their skill. Investing on your own could pose similar conflicts. Your own emotions and subjective thoughts get in the way of making objective decisions.

In addition, the media tends to report only certain stock indexes, such as the Dow Jones Industrial Average, which comprises only thirty stocks; the Standard & Poors (S&P) 500 Index, which contains—you guessed it—only five hundred stocks; or the NASDAQ, which represents about thirty-two hundred stocks. As a result, they ignore many other categories of stock investing such as small capitalization (or "small cap," which means small company stocks), value stocks, and various subcategories of international stocks.

During the so-called Lost Decade of stock investing that took place from 2000 to 2009, the S&P 500 Index was down an average of −1 percent *per year*, which was headline news. On the other hand, what didn't make the front page was the fact that small cap stocks returned +5 percent per year during the same period.[11] Thus it was *not* a "Lost Decade" for small cap stocks. There were certainly a couple of years when small caps suffered severe declines in value. Overall, however, people who didn't panic earned the higher return rate for the decade.

---

11. S&P 500 represented by the Vanguard 500 Index mutual fund and Small Growth represented by the DFA Small Cap Growth mutual fund.

	S&P 500	Small Growth
2000	−9.06%	2.45%
2001	−12.02%	12.79%
2002	−22.15%	−21.16%
2003	28.50%	52.30%
2004	10.74%	17.74%
2005	4.77%	6.87%
2006	15.75%	16.05%
2007	5.47%	−2.35%
2008	−36.97%	−37.22%
2009	26.55%	31.30%
Average Annual Return	−1.00%	+5.01%

When an Irrational Fear of Investing Is Rational

Every day, I help skittish clients work through their aversion to investing. "I trusted my brother-in-law with my life, but I totally lost my shirt when I followed his stock tips," a client will share.

Just because you trust someone to babysit your kids or watch your home while you're away doesn't mean that you should follow his or her investment advice. If you previously ignored the fundamental principles of investing by assuming too much risk; by buying stocks, real estate, gold, and even long-term Treasury bonds when their prices were high; or by pouring your money into something that you didn't thoroughly research or understand, then your fear of making catastrophic mistakes is understandable, but you can't allow it to prevent you from sensible investing. At the same time, it's critical to prudently use your fear as a means to move forward. That is, you learn from your errors, and you then become a better steward of your wealth. On the other hand, if you take your bad experience and throw the investing baby out with the bathwater, you could safely go broke before you die.

Educate Yourself

If concepts like **asset allocation** and **modern portfolio theory** are completely foreign to you, it's time to do your homework. I'll provide an explanation of these terms in the Toolbox at the end of this book. For now, what you need to know is that you *cannot and should not* believe everything your friends, family, coworkers, and the media tell you about investing. Their advice can be extremely difficult to ignore, especially during periods of severe market turbulence when you're hearing reports forecasting the imminent doom of companies whose stock you own, the stock market overall, the economy, and even our nation as a whole. In his book *Investment Policy,* Charles D. Ellis wrote: "Another all-too-human characteristic of most investors is paying too close attention to the day-to-day—even hour-to-hour—ups and downs of stock prices."

The author refers to the ups and downs of prices as "noise or almost random fluctuations." He then recommends that when you find yourself getting swept up in the manic swings of the market to *take a break*. This could mean going for a walk in order to cool off. If you succumb to market excitement or panic, you're essentially following the herd. As a result, you'll make the same mistakes that everyone else makes, which could be catastrophic.[12] The bottom line? Avoid the crowd because *if the crowd was always right, then they'd be rich.*

As Aesop put it long before the Information Age, "Better to be wise by the misfortunes of others than our own." One of the reasons independent **fee-only** investment advisors can add value is that they've witnessed and learned from the mistakes of others.[13] Furthermore, these professionals take your *entire situation* into account, which means that they examine your taxes, future cash flow, income, expenses, assets, goals, estate planning, and more. This comprehensive assessment is critical because individual investment decisions should *never* occur in a vacuum.

Five Investing Tips from a Former Goldman Sachs Broker

Gordan Murray knew that he wanted to publish his book before he died.[14] As I write the words that you're reading right now, I can relate to his commitment to help people. Unlike him, I haven't been diagnosed with brain cancer and given only months to live. Despite a limited amount of time to accomplish his goal, he and his longtime colleague and friend, Daniel C. Goldie, collaborated and completed *The Investment Answer* while he

---

12. Charles D. Ellis, *Investment Policy* (Homewood, Ill.: Business One Irwin, 1985 and 1993).

13. Ron Ross, *The Unbeatable Market* (Ashland, Ohio: BookMasters, Inc., 2002) 212.

14. "A Dying Banker's Last Instructions," *The New York Times*, November 26, 2010.

was still alive. Thankfully he was able to see all twenty thousand copies of his self-published book sell out before his January 2011 death.[15]

I highly recommend that you buy the book. In *The Investment Answer*, Murray, who was a former Goldman Sachs bond salesman and managing director of both Lehman Brothers and Credit Suisse First Boston, provides a powerful guide to investing packaged in a remarkably short work. In part of the book, he and his coauthor highlight five investment guidelines to follow:[16]

1. Hire a fee-only financial advisor.
2. Separate your investments into three groups: stocks and bonds, large and small companies, and value and growth strategies.
3. After following step 2, decide what percentage should be in foreign and domestic investments.
4. Determine whether you'll invest in active or passively managed funds. Prefer low-cost funds over high-cost ones.
5. Continually rebalance, which means that you regularly review your investments, and then shave off some of your winners and buy more of the losers. Yes, you read that right. This may run completely contrary to what you think or feel you should do, but it is absolutely the right thing to do (see **rebalancing** in the Toolbox for more information).

15. "Gordon Murray, Retired Wall Street Executive, Dies at 60; Wrote Investment Guide," *The New York Times*, January 20, 2011
16. Daniel C. Goldie and Gordon S. Murray, *The Investment Answer* (New York: Business Plus, 2011).

Proper Perspective Is Key to Financial Peace of Mind

In order for your portfolio to outlive you, and not the other way around, you need to maintain a long-term perspective, have proper asset allocation, periodically rebalance back to your desired allocation, and *never withdraw excessively* from your portfolio. Violate any one of these tenets, and your life will most likely last longer than your money.

In the next chapter, we'll address what to do when you find that you're withdrawing excessively from your portfolio or when your portfolio plummets in value. I'll also provide a powerful case study that will inspire you to take charge of your financial life.

Chapter 6

Taking Responsibility

Your success in investing will depend in part on your character and guts, and in part on your ability to realize, at the height of ebullience and the depth of despair alike, that this, too, shall pass.
—John Bogle, former chairman of Vanguard Funds

In conflict resolution workshops across the country, participants learn how to use "I" statements, which are a way to express one's feelings without placing blame on others. More importantly, "I" statements encourage the person delivering the message to take ownership of what he or she says.

"I" statements contrast with "You" statements, which both blame and pass responsibility onto others. An example of a "You" statement would be something like, "You didn't meet the project deadline!" The same message expressed with an "I" statement would be, "I'm going to be behind schedule because the project isn't done yet."

In this chapter, you'll learn about the Three Financial "I" Statements. If you find yourself in a financial pinch, I'm certain that you'll be able to identify with at least one of these. How can I state this with such confidence? After more than a quarter of a century in this business, I've provided financial advice to hundreds of individuals; nearly all of those who have money management problems come to me as a result of one or more of the Financial "I" Statements.

Once you've assumed full responsibility for your present state—warts and all—you've taken what's often the most difficult first step, which is to reassess your current predicament with utmost honesty. The next two steps are to reallocate and then recommit.

Financial "I" Statement 1: I Thought I Could Invest on My Own, but Now I Know I Need Help

You may realize that you cannot take an objective look at your current situation because the emotions are overwhelming. This is where a caring yet emotionally detached CFP® Professional will help. I vividly recall an initial consultation I had in 2003 with a husband and wife. They arrived at my office on the heels of the 2000 to 2003 bear market. When I asked why they reached out to me, Carol didn't mince words: "Jim *thought* he could invest our money, but we had to learn the hard way that he shouldn't be doing that, and I don't want him to do it anymore!"

Although harshly criticizing yourself or others for bad decision-making is easy to do, you should avoid this. By refusing to play the financial blame game, you can better assess what you did wrong, and you'll have more clarity regarding how you landed in your current fiscal pit. As a result, you'll be able to effectively address your financial problems.

For example, you may reflect on your losses and think to yourself, "Investing in the stock market was a bad idea." In other words, you're blaming the stock market for your **portfolio's** dip in value. This is most likely an inaccurate assessment. Allow me to suggest the following scenarios, in the form of stock market "I" statements:

1. I invested too much money in a single stock, which meant that I wasn't properly diversified.
2. I bought stocks at a time when prices were high and then sold them when prices were low.
3. I invested too much in stocks and not enough in cash equivalents and bonds.
4. I invested too much in a particular subcategory of stocks and not enough in other subcategories. For example, I overly invested in *large cap* US stocks and not enough in small cap US stocks or international stocks.

> Large cap (capitalization) stocks are very big corporations; small cap stocks are small companies.

You can also substitute the words "real estate" for "stocks" for points 1 to 3.

Even the Industry's Best Often Get It Wrong

"In this business if you're good, you're right six times out of ten. You're never going to be right nine times out of ten." This is a quote from Peter Lynch, former manager of the Fidelity Magellan fund, who amassed one of the best investing track records in the history of **mutual funds**.

He was a top performer, yet a 60 percent success rate was the best he expected. That means that the industry's most respected experts are *wrong 40 percent of the time*. These über-successful pros are the equivalent of professional golfers, which means that there are only a handful of them who win consistently. Even among the fund management elite, very few can even come close to Lynch's track record. In fact, most of them do not beat the index for their particular style of investing. In one of his books, Lynch stated, "All the time and effort that people devote to picking the right fund, the hot hand, the great manager, have in most cases led to no advantage."[17]

So my question to you is, "Do you think you can do better on your own? Really?"

TV's Talking Heads Don't Get It Right Either

Jim Cramer is host of CNBC's *Mad Money*. His show is devoted to helping viewers pick stocks. Eric Tyson, author of *Investing for Dummies* and *Personal Finance for Dummies*, studies Cramer's **stock selection** track record. Overall, after subtracting trading fees, Cramer's selections have performed *worse* than the broad market averages. Tyson said, "The most recent tally shows that out of fifteen hundred stock recommendations, more than half have gone down."[18]

In one rather infamous 2007 case, Cramer recommended Bear Stearns stock, which was selling at $118.20 per share. Shortly after, the firm collapsed and was sold in a fire sale to J.P. Morgan Chase. If you followed his advice on that stock in 2007 and then sold your shares in 2008, they would have gone for $6, which means that you would have lost 95 percent of your investment. I'm not making this point to disparage Cramer. I'm saying this to illustrate that his slightly less than 50 percent success rate isn't that far off from Peter Lynch's assertion that

---

17. Peter Lynch, *Beating the Street* (New York: Simon & Schuster, 1993), 60.
18. Ben Popken, "Jim Cramer's Advice Slightly Worse Than A Coin Toss?" The Consumerist, December 23, 2008, http://consumerist.com/2008/12/jim-cramers-advice-slightly-worse-than-a-coin-toss.html.

the industry's best are right no more than 60 percent of the time. According to Lynch's definition, *Cramer is one of the best stock pickers!*

After years of trying to beat the market by selecting top performing managers for my clients' accounts, and then observing that very few of the managers continued to do better than the benchmark, I finally "got religion" over a decade ago. That's to say that I realized it was better to own the benchmarks rather than to try and find gurus to beat them, let alone pick stocks myself in an attempt to outperform the industry leaders. More on this later in the Toolbox (see **asset allocation, investment choices,** and stock selection).

You may be thinking, "If people like Cramer are among the best, why is their performance not as good as the market averages?" That's precisely my point—most of the excellent managers do not beat the index. They may beat their benchmark one year or even several years in a row, but consistently and persistently for the rest of your life? The answer is no.

Beat the market? Charles D. Ellis, author of *Investment Policy*, observes the following: "It can be done. And it has been done by *most* investors *some* of the time [emphasis mine]. But very few investors have been able to . . . beat the market consistently over the long-term."[19]

Economic historian and publisher Gary North once quipped, "Some extremely sharp investment advisors can get you in at the bottom of the market. Some extremely sharp ones can get you out at the top. They are never the same people!"

---

19. Charles D. Ellis, *Investment Policy* (Homewood, Ill.: Business One Irwin, 1985), 11.

Financial "I" Statement 2: I Trusted Someone that I Shouldn't Have

For many years, I've been treasurer of my local Kiwanis club. When I first joined, there was another member who, like me, was a financial advisor. He had gained the respect and trust of key members before I came on board. By the time I joined, many had already given him their money to manage.

I knew that I could serve my fellow club members' financial needs just as well as he could, with the exception of one important matter. He delivered consistently high investment returns with a low degree of risk. It was a combination that I couldn't match. From the start, I was very skeptical of his investment methods, and later my suspicions proved right.

The federal government investigated his business and eventually sent him to prison for running a Ponzi scheme. This is where a swindler provides returns on a client's investments that are paid for by new investors who hand their money over to the crook. It often falls apart when there aren't enough new funds coming in to support the returns promised to earlier investors. If you've heard of one of these before, it's probably thanks to Bernard Madoff, the investment advisor whose scam fell apart in 2008 and earned him a 150-year prison term. Madoff will forever be known for running the largest Ponzi scheme in US history. It's widely been reported to have been a $65 billion heist. Madoff proves that as long as there's money to be made, you'll find swindlers and charlatans in any profession. They appeal to investors' greed and desire for consistently high returns with no risk, *which is never possible.*

Past Performance Doesn't Guarantee Future Results

On a less deceptive note, some advisors will pitch certain investment managers or mutual funds to you based on terrific twelve-month or three-year returns. They'll show you fancy brochures that advertise facts that aren't false or deceptive. The marketing materials present a compelling case to the novice investor. One of the biggest pitfalls to investing in mutual funds like these, however, is that you end up buying when prices are high. To avoid this, it's important to realize that unlike an interest rate on a bank CD, a mutual fund's prior results don't tell you anything about what will happen over the next twelve months, let alone the next three years. Furthermore, when it comes to your investments, *it's the long-term that matters, not the short-term.* So, if three years isn't long-term, how many years is?

The economist John Maynard Keynes famously said, "In the long run, we're all dead." My mantra is "five years, five years, five years!" If you cannot leave your money invested for at least half a decade, it should not be put in anything but bank accounts or short-term bond funds. For serious investors, Keynes's observation speaks the truth; long-term is your life expectancy. In other words, it's the rest of your life.

Financial "I" Statement 3:
I Was Too Greedy

You may have been one of the millions of Americans who, between the years 1997 and 2006, hopped on the real estate bandwagon as real estate values climbed to euphoric heights. Perhaps you convinced yourself that the real estate bull market would charge upward forever. As a result, you "flipped" multiple properties by signing up for loans with terms that in hindsight were absurd.

Most of us have a "get rich quick" gene inside us. The impulse to succumb to our genetic predisposition is stronger in some than in others. What often intensifies our money-hungry DNA is the risk versus return relationship. Low risk translates to low returns, and high risk can yield high returns or huge losses. We may convince ourselves that the high risk of a particular investment is the price we must pay in order to potentially strike gold.

Note that there is one combination of investment returns that should *never* be believed: high returns and low risk. If someone suggests something like this, run—don't walk—for the nearest exit. Otherwise, you'll have to learn about risk the hard way.

Life after the Financial "I" Statements

Now that we've diagnosed the problem, we're ready to move forward. So what do you do if you've sustained a hit to your portfolio that keeps you up at night? Depending on the particular assets that you've invested in, you might be able to wait for a recovery. In the worst-case scenario, however, you may never get back your investment. Even if it was completely wiped out, there is a silver lining around this dark fiscal cloud. The solution is simple: You really have no choice but to put it behind you and move forward. Next you have to figure out how to add as much as possible to your savings and investments, *right now.*

This assumes that you're still employed or at least employable. If you're already retired and will not or cannot go back to work, your only options are to significantly reduce your spending, sell some other assets, or both. For most retirees, the answer is to cut spending. I am painfully aware that no one wants to cut back spending—especially the US government, but that's a completely different book. Dramatically reducing spending is a bitter pill that you must take in order to heal. When I mention this to clients, their reactions range from mild discomfort to angry denial. So imagine my surprise when a client shared what she and her husband had done *voluntarily* to slash their budget. The following is her true story.

Case Study: Buried Under Debt, a Client Emerges Happier than Ever

If someone had told me five years ago that I'd be where I am today, I would have said, "No way!" Back then, my husband and I were in the midst of a financial meltdown. We had five cars, a boat, four houses, and a lot of headaches. I had to move money around every month to cover various mortgages. When my husband and I took an honest look at the money management mess, we realized that in order to reign in our out-of-control expenses, we needed to be able to reasonably predict our expenses and manage them. The next step was to simplify our lives.

Now, five years later, we have two cars that we actually own free and clear, and one wonderful house with a low, secure mortgage. The process of getting our financial house in order took several years, and I'll share exactly how we did it.

The First Year: Cutting Monthly Costs by $5,000

After the 2008 market downturn, I realized that I needed to begin tracking our expenditures. That way, I could better understand where our money was going. So in January 2009, I started recording our weekly expenses in an Excel spreadsheet. I saw that my husband and I spent $11,500 in January and $14,000 in February. During those two months, I sold a property that my father had left me, and I used the proceeds to pay off our home equity line of credit. By closely monitoring and then controlling our expenses, we were able to reduce our monthly costs to $9,000 by May.

In the same way that maintaining a food log assists in weight loss, looking at what we spent each month helped us to lose inches off our financial waistline. The benefits of our new approach to money management were so significant that in June, we decided to simplify even more: we canceled our housekeeper (it was a little painful, but we saved almost $4,000 per year), signed up for a family cell phone plan, shopped around to reduce our health insurance premiums, and more.

Twelve Months Later, We're Spending 20 Percent Less Overall

By December 2009 our spending was down to $8,000 a month. For the whole year, we spent $125,000, which represented a savings of $25,000, or 20 percent less than we spent in 2008. Monitoring our expenses actually became fun. We looked at every major expense and asked ourselves how it could be trimmed. At the same time, we insisted on maintaining our quality of life and continued to fulfill our commitment to assist family members.

In late 2009, I set a budget of $85,000 for 2010. That's $40,000, or 30 percent, less than we spent in 2009, and probably more like 40 percent less than in 2008 and prior years. The new budget covered all major expense categories adequately and even left a few thousand dollars for emergencies.

As I write these words, we will be on budget nearly to the penny. No sweating and no suffering. Instead my husband I are enjoying life, traveling, eating out, having fun, going to concerts, and giving gifts. We have all the same television channels and better cell phones, eat out whenever we want to, and live in a warm house with happy furry kids (some people call them pets). We are actually having more fun because we're finding it utterly fulfilling to take control of our finances. We're saving despite planning a fabulous thirteen-day vacation to Paris, Athens, and the Greek Islands. Through our travel research, we've learned about great online tools like Priceline.com. As a result, our European vacation will cost us only $7,000. I can't believe that in 2008, we spent $15,000 on a ten-day vacation to Italy. In 2009, we didn't even plan a major trip because we couldn't afford it; this year we'll take two or three.

Simplify, Simplify, Simplify!

The process of drastically reducing our spending wasn't easy at first. And it did take focus, but now we enjoy taking advantage of all the ways we can save money. None of these are secrets; we just never bothered to use them. It's as simple as asking for a discount before renewing the next two-year mobile phone contract—that saved us $360 a year. It's using Priceline.com—I bid for and won a $65 hotel room that was listed for $240 on the hotel website. I cleaned out our basement and netted over $2,000 in one weekend by hopping on Craigslist and selling our belongings (I used some of the proceeds to spoil myself with an iPad). Our savings plan allowed us to also give a nice chunk of change to help the parents of our new niece. We bought a used car for another niece. We continue to max out our frequent flyer program points. We have joined a couple of loyalty programs with our favorite restaurants, which, on occasion, earn us free lunches. We pay for known expenses with prepaid gift cards we buy at a discount, and clip a few coupons here and there for our most frequently purchased items (we're saving $400 on soy milk this year alone!). Not one of these steps is difficult to do anymore, and all of them pay off—*big time*!

By now, I'm pretty sure that this new behavior is a permanent part of our lives. I used to waste money—a lot of it. I'm confident that those days are over. *This is just much more fun.*

There was a time when I dreamed of having a lot of money and a lavish lifestyle to go with it. But I don't need that now. I've adjusted, let go of those lofty thoughts, and found ways to be truly happy—and exceedingly grateful—for everything *we really have.* We live just as well, give just as much to family, friends, and charity, and do it on a whole lot less. This makes us much more secure about our future.

My husband and I are convinced that we're finally prepared for the next phase of our lives together. We are clearer on what we want and don't want, and we realize what we need to be happy. *It's a great feeling.* It took several years to get where we are today, but it was well worth the effort.

The following are some websites that helped in our saving process:

- www.bidcactus.com
- www.kayak.com
- www.hotwire.com
- www.priceline.com
- www.craigslist.com

For more **general money management tips,** see the Toolbox.

What Is Asset Allocation?

In this section, I'll show you how to reallocate your investments. Once you learn the asset allocation basics, you must vow to do whatever it takes to learn from past mistakes.

The most important judgment call you, as an investor, will make is the asset allocation decision. Asset allocation is a relatively new phrase that came into vogue after the 1986 Brinson, Hood, and Beebower study[20] of ninety-one large pension plans. The study concluded that more than 90 percent of the variation in these plans' performance could be attributed to their asset allocation policy and *not* to stock picking or market timing. Asset allocation is strategically designing a portfolio using the following steps:

> You may also hear the term "**diversification.**" Asset allocation is an organized and scientific method of diversification.

1. Deciding which asset categories (stocks, bonds, international, real estate, commodities, etc.) will be included in the portfolio

2. Determining the target allocation percentage for each asset category

3. Specifying the acceptable range for the deviation from the target percentage and committing to **rebalancing** back to the target when any category rises or falls out of the range

4. Selecting managers for each asset category

The first two steps form the foundation for the portfolio's risk versus return characteristics.[21]

Even if you don't think you're allocating your assets, you probably are. For example, imagine that you've decided to avoid the stock market. Therefore you have all of your money tied

---

19. Gary P. Brinson, L. Randolph Hood, and Gilbert L. Beebower, "Determinants of Portfolio Performance," *Financial Analysts Journal*, July/August 1986.

21. Roger C. Gibson, *Asset Allocation: Balancing Financial Risk* (Homewood, Ill.: Dow Jones-Irwin, 1990), 8.

up in real estate. This is asset allocation. Or let's say you have 100 percent of your savings in bank CDs and money market funds; this is an example of asset allocation as well. In financial advisor–speak, we would describe the former as a 100 percent allocation to real estate, and the latter as being 100 percent in cash equivalents. When I started in this business in the mid-1980s, 100 percent in cash equivalents was quite common. At the time, bank CDs were paying 9 percent or more in interest, and many people were perfectly content putting all of their money in CDs. The following is a joke that illustrated how widespread this form of investing was:

A woman arranged to meet with a financial advisor. He looked at her portfolio and noticed that she was 100 percent invested in CDs.

"Ma'am, my suggestion is that you diversify," he said.

"But I already am," she answered. "I've got my money in five different banks!"

Having 100 percent of your money in one asset class or category is foolish and downright dangerous. Various courts throughout our country agree. In case law, a concept called the "Prudent Investor Rule" requires that trustees and other fiduciaries diversify investments; usually this means that no more than 6 percent may be invested in any one asset category.

The "Prudent Investor Rule" came about largely from lawsuits within wealthy families. High **net worth** families have historically used trusts to meet a variety of investment, tax, and control objectives. The people in charge of the trusts, called trustees, were sued because they invested in assets that dropped in value, sometimes substantially. Courts would rule in favor of the trustees if they followed prudent investing principles, even if the investments lost money. As an investor, you too should keep in mind the "Prudent Investor Rule" when you're allocating your assets.

Now that I've provided the basics on asset allocation, I'll address reallocation. If you need to make significant changes to your asset allocation, you have two options: do it yourself or hire a professional. In either instance, my recommendation is to use **modern portfolio theory**, or MPT, as your guide. Whether you go it alone or hire a CFP® Professional, you need to consider a specific set of factors so that you can allocate your assets effectively. These factors fall into two broad groups: *objective* and *subjective.*

The objective factors include the following:
- Your age
- How much money you have to invest
- Your tax bracket
- Whether you'll be adding to your portfolio or withdrawing from it in order to supplement your income
- Your years of experience with investing

The subjective factors include the following:
- Your emotional capacity to handle risk and volatility
- How you feel about different investments
- Your susceptibility to listen and respond to investment "noise"—in other words, what friends, family, and the media say
- The reasonableness of your expectations

Are You Ready to Recommit?

It's one thing to say, "I'm going to lose weight by improving my **diet** and **exercising** more." It's an entirely different matter to get out and do it. The same holds true for investing, particularly after a scary period such as the Lost Decade from 2000 to 2009 and the Great Recession of 2008–2009. During the Great Recession, the stock market plummeted more than 50 percent and many people lost substantial amounts or perhaps their entire investment in individual stocks, real estate, or both. After assessing their losses, many reacted like a kid touching a hot stove. They insisted that they would never invest in the market again. Bursting real estate bubbles have created similar responses.

By acknowledging which of the Three Financial "I" Statements describes your current state, you're taking an essential step toward improving your financial life. After all, you can't fix a problem until you acknowledge that one exists. Next, you must reallocate your investments. Finally, you need to recommit. Here's where you will decide whether you're disciplined enough to redouble your efforts and implement your own financial plan or you need to hire an expert. As I pointed out in chapter 5, the DALBAR study showed that over a twenty-year period, the average investor didn't even beat inflation with his dismal 2.3 percent return. It's important to consider whether or not working with a CFP® Professional, who is objective and possesses specific knowledge, will help you make better decisions than you would on your own. Now that you've moved beyond excuses and toward meeting bigger and better goals, you need to follow the Nike slogan and "Just do it!"

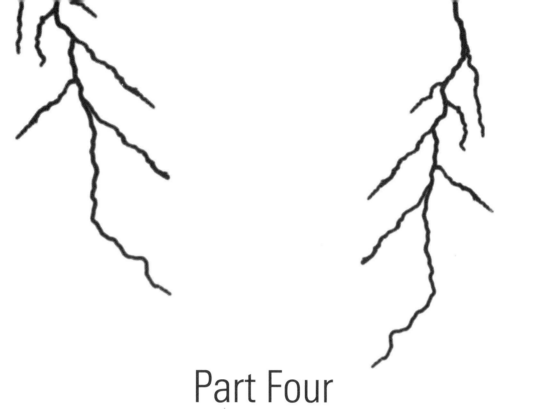

Part Four

What If I Lost My Marriage?

Chapter 7

Prevention and Protection

"For I hate divorce," says the LORD, the God of Israel.
—Malachi 2:16

I knew a man who was going through a divorce. It was one of those bitter breakups that you've probably witnessed friends or family experience—maybe you have endured the awful experience yourself. There was a hostile custody battle over a son, combat between dueling lawyers over assets big and small, and tens of thousands in legal costs. What made the experience even harder for him to comprehend was that he knew he was a reasonable and level-headed person. After the breakup, it required years to get his financial house back in order, but it took even more time to heal from the emotional scars of the marriage's messy end. How do I know the intimate details of this divorce? Because this is what happened to me.

Divorce is the death of one of life's most precious relationships. That's why it can be as psychologically and financially devastating as the death of a spouse. I'm sure you've heard the sad statistics.

Roughly half of all marriages end in divorce, and the financial consequences can be disastrous. Most people, especially women, wind up in dire financial straits unless they were married to a wealthy spouse with a high income and they were together for a long time. For mothers with small children, divorce can be a woman's worst nightmare. Single moms have to juggle a job and raising kids, and having to worry about receiving child support makes matters even worse. It's no exaggeration to say that being a single mom is the world's toughest job.

Regardless of whether you're a man or a woman, rarely do either of the ex-spouses come out financially better than if they'd stayed together. Personal experience and years of working with divorced clients have convinced me that divorce is one of the biggest financial mistakes anyone can make. In this chapter, I'll begin by showing how to prevent a marriage from breaking up. Then I'll spend the rest of the chapter helping you deal with the reality of a divorce.

Planning Ahead

Money and sex. These two themes not only drive the world of news and entertainment but also are the main causes of divorce. With that said, the best planning that a couple can do to avoid divorce has little to do with the money part. It's more about communication. Communication is an essential characteristic of a successful marriage, even in its less warm and fuzzy forms, such as arguing or expressing frustration, anger, or unhappiness. Without solid communication, individuals may find themselves like a deer in the headlights when their husband or wife demands a divorce.

"Cal, I had no idea it was coming," a client will tell me. The downcast spouse sits across from me, reeling in shock over the news—still in denial about his or her spouse's desire to divorce. I often follow up by asking, "What was the level of communication between both of you?" My clients' responses typically lie somewhere between "nonexistent" and "really bad." That explains why clients often tell me they didn't know anything was wrong.

Divorce Advice from a Self-Professed Nonexpert

In addition to the possible financially catastrophic consequences of divorce, there are several other solid reasons for making a marriage work. Avoiding the emotional impact on children, the injury to your self-esteem, depression, and trust issues are just a few examples.

My specialty is in finance and taxes—and I have all of the official titles and advanced degrees to prove it. I am no expert in marriage counseling. If anything, I'm an expert in how to do it wrong! Then again, I got it right the second time. My second wife and I have been happily married for more than twenty years.

Since I'm not a psychologist or a marriage and family therapist, I tread lightly when it comes to providing relationship advice. What I will share are some resources that have worked for many people, as well as my wife and me. The bestselling book *Men Are from Mars, Women Are from Venus* highlights the differences between men and women, and the author provides insights into how to effectively bridge the gap. Two other books that have guided me are *His Needs, Her Needs* by psychologist William Harley and *The 5 Love Languages: The Secret to Love that Lasts* by Gary Chapman. My wife and I have also benefited immensely from church seminars and "Weekend to Remember" events sponsored by Family Life Ministries, a Christian organization. You can find them online at www.familylife.com.

Both reading self-help books and attending marriage seminars point to one important aspect of making a marriage work: it requires time and effort. Improving communication between you and your spouse is a never-ending work in progress. Think of a healthy relationship as you would physical fitness. If you **exercise** regularly and maintain a healthy **diet**, your overall health will benefit. What if you reached a certain fitness or weight goal, and you stopped putting forth any more effort? Your health would probably deteriorate. Marriage is similar. A good marriage takes work. You must consistently spend time together and work as a team. Neglect your marriage, and you run the risk of ruining it. Now that I've touched on the emotional aspects of planning ahead, we'll explore the legal aspects.

Prenuptial Agreements Can Ruin a Romance and Protect Your Assets

A prenuptial agreement, also called a prenup or a premarital agreement, is a contract that is effective prior to your marriage. The prenup's provisions can vary widely, but it commonly outlines the division of property and spousal support if you divorce. It may also include terms for the forfeiture of assets as a result of a marriage breakup that takes place because of adultery.

If you're looking for one surefire way to spoil a romantic dinner, say the following: "Honey, let's talk prenups." Bring it up kindly, aggressively, gently, or full of hostility—it doesn't matter. Most likely, the person on the other side of the table will respond to your suggestion with a sudden "Waiter, check please!" because it indicates a lack of trust.

For the first marriage, I generally tell my clients that a prenuptial agreement is a bad idea. One exception might be if one of you has built up or inherited substantial wealth and seeks to protect it. In most states, however, simply keeping *premarital assets* registered or titled in your name alone and not retitling them as joint tenants can protect them. If this is documented and the assets aren't comingled, then they are often not subject to division in a divorce.

> Premarital assets are assets brought into the marriage by each person that were accumulated prior to the marriage.

In addition to *not* being a relationship expert, I'm no attorney either. Because I'm not qualified to dispense legal advice, it's best that you consult a family law attorney in your state. He or she will provide guidance that will address the particular laws where you live and your specific circumstances.

So when do I recommend a premarital agreement? Rarely. During a second marriage, however, there are certain times when it may be appropriate. First, for people in their forties and over who are remarrying and have adult children, typically a discussion about a prenup is not a deal-breaker or unromantic—in fact, it's expected and prudent. Second, if there's accumulated wealth, as I described in the previous paragraph, it's a good idea to discuss this openly, especially if you have children from your first marriage. This is because you must be very careful not to unintentionally disinherit your kids. This advice pertains to remarriage after widowhood as well as divorce.

For example, if you simply remarried and then retitled all your assets jointly with your new spouse and then died, who would get your money? It would all go to your new spouse, not your kids. Remember, as I explained in chapter 1, joint tenancy trumps your will. The same would be true if you named your new spouse the primary **beneficiary** of your IRA or **life insurance**. You have to be very careful with all of these decisions.

Instead of a prenup, you could revise or amend your **revocable living trust** to specify what would happen to your various assets if you predeceased your new spouse. You could even name your trust as the primary beneficiary of your IRA or life insurance. Again, this is when you should contact an attorney because this is the professional who will draft the contract or trust and answer your questions with full knowledge of the laws pertaining to your state. A good CFP® Professional will periodically review your beneficiary designations, asset **titling**, and trust distribution language to make absolutely certain your loved ones do not get disinherited.

If the Saying, "Shoot the Messenger" Applies to You, Have Your Advisor Take the Arrow

Consider counting on your CFP® Professional to be the bearer of bad news. In this good cop–bad cop scenario, your advisor will be the one who brings up the importance of having a prenuptial agreement or amending the trust. I've done this many times for my clients, particularly those with financially complex, high **net worth** estates. During our meeting, I reveal the benefits of a prenup and the consequences that may result from inaction. Because I'm a third-party participant in the discussion, my clients avoid looking like the bad guys. This also prevents those who are hearing my recommendation from feeling like their future spouses don't trust them.

Premarital Agreements in the Real World

Example 1

Kathleen was sixty-two years old when she married Jerry, who had just celebrated his sixty-fifth birthday. This was the second marriage for both of them. The couple decided that both Kathleen and Jerry would sell their houses and together buy a new luxury condominium. They hired an attorney, who drafted a premarital agreement. It stated that if either one of them died, the surviving spouse retained the right to live in the house and take care of all the expenses. After the survivor died, however, the house would be sold and the proceeds, which might be $750,000 or more after paying off the mortgage, would be divided according to the percentage of the equity Kathleen and Jerry had put into the house. Then they would be distributed to all of the children from both of their previous marriages according to the provisions of their trusts.

Example 2

Like Jerry and Kathleen, it was Julie and Keith's second marriage. Keith sold his house and moved in with Julie. She owned her house free and clear. Keith did not put any of the money he received from the sale of his house into Julie's house; he kept it in a separate trust account with his kids as beneficiaries.

The couple worked with an attorney who added a provision to both Julie's and Keith's trusts. It gave Keith the right to continue to live in the house if Julie died first. He could also sell it and buy another house of equal or lesser value. If, at the time of Julie's death, the house was worth $1 million, Keith could put it on the market and buy another house for that amount or less. If Keith sold it later for $1.5 million and bought another house for $1 million, the children from Julie's previous marriage would be entitled to the $500,000 difference. Once Keith died, the house would go to Julie's children. In addition, her kids would receive all of her assets and the inheritance she had originally acquired from her parents. Keith, in turn, was the sole beneficiary of her $1 million life insurance policy.

These two examples illustrate how a well-crafted agreement can accommodate nearly any circumstance or desire. If you work with an experienced family law or estate planning attorney, he or she will most likely have successfully handled situations similar to yours. The lawyer's skill will guide you and help you determine the proper language to use in order to draft a premarital plan that protects your interests.

Dealing with Reality

Let's say you find yourself on the unfortunate side of the marriage statistic. Although you've done everything in your power to prevent a breakup, it's time for a divorce. In this section, you'll see how a client of mine successfully navigated the precarious divorce waters. Let her experience be your guide.

Eva's parents had been my clients for years. Although I hadn't worked with Eva directly, her parents suggested that she give me a call when she told them she was getting a divorce. When Eva and I met in my office, she told me she had heard plenty of divorce horror stories, and her goal was to avoid the same fate.

"I want this to be over and done with as soon as possible. My husband and I are getting along fine, and I think we can handle this on our own," she said.

As hopeful as she was, I knew the complexities that could arise during a divorce. So before I supported her plan, I took a quick inventory of her marital estate.

"Do you know if he has any retirement accounts and how much he has in each?" I asked.

"I know he has something, but I really don't know what that *something* is . . . or the amount," she said.

"You shared that he has his own business. How long has he had it?" I asked.

"He started it right after we married," she said.

I let her know that a lawyer might recommend a **business valuation** to determine how much of it she would be entitled to. She didn't know what a business valuation was. When I

> Business valuation is a determination of how much a business is worth if sold or divided up and split among its owners.

explained it to her and why it was important, the news surprised her.

"Where do you envision your kids living? How much would you need every month to meet their needs?" I asked.

Eva hadn't deeply considered matters such as child custody and support. I continued to inquire about her marital estate. I found out that she had worked prior to becoming a stay-at-home mom and had contributed to a 401(k) throughout her employment. She had also received an inheritance from her grandfather.

"I know I'm going to sound completely naive when I say this, but I'd been so preoccupied with the emotional stress of the divorce that I hadn't given much thought to the financial impact," she said.

Eva was an educated, responsible woman. Like many at the onset of the dissolution of a marriage though, she realized that the words "I want a divorce" and the way the process would actually play out were essentially two unrelated matters.

One is a seemingly straightforward statement of intent, while the actual sorting out of details is a very technical matter, which is *especially the case* for high net worth marital estates. For Eva and her husband, the business valuation had the potential to be in the millions and his retirement account values were unknown and could be huge. By the end of our meeting, she understood that for every emotional consequence of divorce, there would be an equal or greater financial burden. Although I had provided her valuable insight, I made certain that she knew my advice could only address the financial matters of her marital estate. If she wanted answers to her legal concerns, she had to meet with a lawyer. At the meeting's end, Eva decided to contact a family law attorney.

What's the Role of a Divorce Lawyer?

In some divorces, the spouses are able to work out issues amicably. The attorney merely drafts their divorce agreement following the terms the divorcing couple has agreed to. Also, there is a relatively new type of divorce process called "Collaborative Divorce." A friend of mine in Georgia used this process and was quite satisfied with it. The process includes attorneys, counselors, and financial planners. More information is available at www.collaborativepracticega.com.

> Alimony is an annual payment from one divorced spouse to the other ex-spouse. The dollar amount and number of years to be paid must be specified in the divorce agreement to meet tax law requirements.

After Eva shared basic details of her marital estate, however, I could tell that her case would be far from do-it-yourself. There were many factors involved: their children, her husband's business, their separate retirement accounts, income she generated before she quit her job, and of course child support and *alimony*.

"How do I find a lawyer?" she asked.

I suggested that she speak with her trusted friends and family members and see if they could provide referrals. I knew several attorneys, and because she lived in the community where I worked, I was able to refer her to a good family lawyer.

"But whatever you do, don't cut corners," I insisted. In my experience, the saying "You get what you pay for" can sometimes be a shallow justification to buy some luxury item you lust for. However, that phrase usually holds true for family law attorneys. Effective divorce negotiation could mean the difference between a parent maintaining custody of his or her children versus losing custody, being awarded alimony that leaves a husband or wife feeling satisfied rather than exploited, or receiving hundreds of thousands or even millions of dollars—a fair share of the marital estate—as opposed to being taken to the cleaners. Spending a few thousand dollars more for excellent representation is an investment with a potentially massive payoff.

Early in my career, I witnessed a client lose custody of her kids and have to pay child support to her ex-husband. It wasn't that she was a bad mother; it was simply a result of her poor decision to hire an inexpensive lawyer who was not a specialist in family law. In the end, her decision to pay $500 for a lawyer instead of the $5,000 retainer that the so-called overpriced attorney required, paled in comparison to the long-term costs— both emotional and financial—of inadequate legal counsel.

"Any last words of advice?" Eva asked.

"Start off fighting hard for your rights. Later, if your ex is cooperative and amicable, you can ease up," I said. I added that she should begin with the premise of getting as much as she was legally entitled to. A good lawyer would point out what was proper and reasonable to expect given the laws of their state.

Eva appreciated my guidance, and she ended up hiring me as her CFP® Professional. As her divorce proceeded, she worked with her attorney and regularly asked me to explain the financial intricacies of dividing their marital estate.

How the Courts Grant Child Support and Alimony

Many states have adopted formulas or grids to determine child support. This creates more consistency (less subjectivity in judges' decisions) in the amounts the courts grant. The formulas consider the income of the husband and wife, as well as the number of children they have.

As a tax expert, I emphasize the tax consequences of certain provisions. *Child support isn't tax deductible to the paying spouse and it isn't taxable income to the receiving spouse.* The dependency deduction for each child is typically granted to the custodial spouse, which is the one with whom the children live most of the time. However, this can be negotiated and given to the noncustodial spouse as well. If the custodial parent does not have much taxable income, it's really a waste for that person to take the dependents' deduction. In order for this alternative arrangement to be recognized, it must be stated in the divorce decree. Also, IRS Form 8332, "Release/Revocation of Release of Claim to Exemption for Child by Custodial Parent," must be filed with the noncustodial parent's tax return annually. In addition, that tax form must be signed by the custodial spouse every year. If the parent is in *Alternative Minimum Tax* (AMT), the dependency exemption can be

> Alternative minimum tax is a separate tax calculation that eliminates many deductions and imposes a flat tax of 26–28 percent. You pay the greater of the regular tax or the alternative minimum tax calculations.

useless. Therefore, if the couple can work it out, it makes sense to give the exemption to the parent who is not in AMT.

In the case of alimony, judges have more latitude. *Alimony is tax deductible for the paying spouse and taxable income to the receiving spouse.* Alimony is based on a number of factors—how long the couple was married, the respective incomes of the spouses, whether one spouse gave up his or her career to raise the kids, and a number of nonfinancial factors, such as cases of adultery and abandonment.

Division of Assets

"My lawyer described that some assets have a tax consequence. Can you help me understand this?" Eva asked.

In the simplest terms, if Eva and her husband's combined marital estate consisted of only a $500,000 house and a $500,000 IRA, and she was younger than fifty-nine-and-a-half, withdrawals from the IRA would be taxable income *plus* there would be a 10 percent tax penalty for early withdrawal. This meant that she needed to carefully examine each asset using the following factors as a guide:

- **Liquidity**—Can it be easily turned into cash?
- **Tax consequences**—For IRAs and other retirement plans, or low basis non-IRA investments, what would the tax hit be if sold?
- **Income-generating potential**—Are there any assets that will continue to produce income for many years? For example, a rental property that produces positive cash flow. On the other hand, a rental property could be cash flow negative (that is, it loses money each year because expenses are greater than the rental income) and would be a fiscal burden for the ex-spouse who receives that

property. This would require serious consideration and negotiation. (I'll be the first to acknowledge that this issue is complicated!)

- **Debt**—Is there a debt or a mortgage associated with the asset, such as in the case of a house, that would make it difficult to keep?
- **Risk**—Is there a likelihood that the asset could substantially decline in value or even become worthless?

Speaking of IRAs, in most cases, an IRA can be divided between you and your ex-spouse without triggering a taxable distribution; you simply provide the signed divorce decree. In other instances, and for other retirement assets, such as a 401(k), you'll need a Qualified Domestic Relations Order (QDRO). Retirement assets that are incorrectly divided can result in substantial tax penalties to you, your ex-spouse, or both of you. You've got to be very careful with these things.

Changing Beneficiaries on IRAs, Other Retirement Accounts, and Life Insurance

"Trust me, you don't want your kids or family members to deal with this situation," I warned Eva. I explained that if she didn't change beneficiaries, and she passed away after the divorce, her ex-spouse would receive all the money. She cringed at the thought.

Excessive Debt Is a Killer

A few years back, a colleague shared this proverb with me: "If your outflow exceeds your income, your upkeep will be your downfall!" In Eva's case, she and her husband had managed their money wisely and her lawyer had skillfully negotiated on her behalf. As a result, her postdivorce life would put her in decent financial shape. That's not to say that it was perfect, but it wasn't dire either. I also knew that she was motivated to make whatever changes were necessary.

In general, when all the negotiating is over, you want as little debt as possible. If, despite your best efforts, you still end up with substantial red ink, you need to immediately work your way out of debt. Not all debts are the same, and some are more hazardous to your financial well-being than others. That's why you need to prioritize your debt elimination process.

If you're uncertain where to even start, I highly recommend that you read Dave Ramsey's *Total Money Makeover*. The author provides a straightforward and effective plan to work your way out of debt. He also has a regular radio program where he answers listeners' questions. To learn more, visit www.daveramsey.com.

Controlling Your Spending

In most marriages, one spouse takes on the daily money management tasks. Once divorced, the other spouse must suddenly assume a role that he or she may not be ready for. This was the case for Eva. We worked together to develop a budget for her new life. First we determined her after-tax income and her monthly expenses. The initial figures came as unwelcome news—her current expenses were higher than her income. To solve the negative cash flow problem she had to consider the following:

1. **Reduce expenses**
2. **Increase income** by getting a job or a better-paying one if she was already employed
3. **Sell assets**

After hearing my financial straight talk, the look on her face made me wonder if she regretted ever meeting with me in the first place.

"I know that this isn't what you wanted to hear. But my main concern is that at your current rate of spending, making ends meet will require you to withdraw excessive amounts from your investment **portfolio**," I said.

As a CFP® Professional, my job was to make sure Eva didn't run out of money before she ran out of life. If, in order to cover her monthly expenses, she had to pull money from her savings, the odds were high that she wouldn't have enough to support herself in the long run.

"It's a bitter pill," she said.

"But the earlier we deal with it, the better. Let me provide you the following scenario," I said.

In the divorce settlement, Eva ended up with an investment portfolio of $1,000,000. During their marriage, her husband had earned a high income, which allowed them to lead an affluent lifestyle. Now that she was divorced, we determined that in order to maintain the same standard of living, she would have to withdraw $100,000 per year from her portfolio, which was 10 percent of its value. This figure also factored in income she received from alimony and what her kids would receive in child support. Assuming that there was no growth in her investments, after one year her portfolio would be worth $900,000. As the Wall Street meltdown in 2008 demonstrated, stock markets could take a sudden plunge. If Eva's portfolio decreased in value 20 percent, her $900,000 savings would now be worth $700,000. The following year, if she withdrew $100,000 to meet her expenses, her portfolio would be worth $600,000. Under these circumstances, it would take a *nearly 70 percent rate of return* in order for her to reach the original $1,000,000 value of her portfolio.

"$1,000,000 sounded like so much money at first. But not anymore," she said.

"The good news is that it is a lot of money. But you've got to control your spending in order for it to last," I said.

Eva was motivated to be the best possible mother to her children and to maintain financial independence. Through our work together she was able to do both successfully.

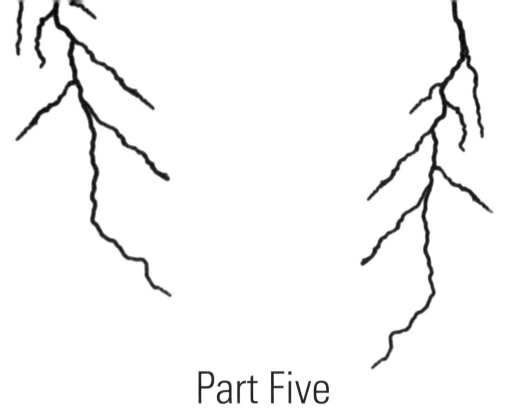

Part Five

What If I Lost My Parents?

Chapter 8

Making Difficult Plans

A man's dying is more the survivors' affair than his own.
—Thomas Mann

When J. Howard Marshall died at age ninety, his two sons assumed that they would inherit his estate. The last thing they anticipated was that taking control of his assets would require fifteen years and be mired in public scandal. In fact, the battle over his estate landed on the steps of the US Supreme Court in the case *Marshall v. Marshall*.

What complicated matters was both their father's massive wealth and the claims made by his third wife—model and TV personality Anna Nicole Smith, who was twenty-six years old when they married. When he passed away fourteen months after they wed, the business magnate was worth $1.6 billion. Anna Nicole insisted that her late husband had promised her $300 million, although this was never documented in his will.

Most likely settling a parent's estate won't be a matter for the Supreme Court to decide. But J. Howard Marshall's story illustrates the issues that arise with second and third marriages, children from different marriages, and high **net worth** estates. In this chapter, I'll describe how to effectively communicate about your parents' estate with them, and the steps you need to take in order to protect their health, their well-being, and their assets.

What Will Life Look Like After My Parents Die?

I speak on behalf of my wife, my son, and myself when I say that losing a parent, whether it's expected or a complete surprise, is one of life's most emotionally painful experiences. For me, my father died at age sixty-nine of a heart attack. My wife's mother passed away in our home when she was eighty-seven years old. She suffered from acute dementia, and she lived with us for the last two years of her life. Sometimes the passing of a parent comes even earlier. My son's mother died when he was only twenty-five years old; she and I had divorced in the late 1980s. In each case, my wife, my son, and I had prepared ahead of time, which provided us financial stability that supported us through our losses.

The Ideal Estate Plan

A successful estate plan will meet the following six objectives:
- Virtually no assets will go through **probate**.
- Minimal to zero **estate taxes** will be paid.
- Minimal income taxes (especially **capital gains**) will be incurred.
- Assets will transfer hassle-free to the appropriate heirs at the appropriate time.

- Assets will be protected from creditors, Uncle Sam, and any irresponsible or mentally challenged heirs.
- No arguments, lawsuits, or disputes will arise among heirs.

So how do you go about meeting these lofty goals? You start by asking yourself a very difficult question: Once your parents die, who will take control of their assets? Your answer will determine how you will communicate with your parents about their estate. Examine the following questions.

1. Will there be a surviving spouse?

If the answer is yes, as an adult child you may have little to do. The surviving spouse will take on the daily tasks of running the household such as paying bills and keeping track of accounts. In the event that he or she is not interested in managing finances or is unable to, you may have to step in.

2. What if there's a surviving spouse from a remarriage and there are children from a previous marriage?

This can lead to complicated inheritance issues that could potentially wind up in the courts, such as what happened to the estate of Anna Nicole Smith's husband. To avoid possible snags, the trusts, **life insurance**, and named beneficiaries of IRAs and retirement plans must be checked and double-checked.

3. What if there's no spouse, either because of a prior death or divorce?

As an adult child, the responsibility rests in your hands. If siblings or other family members are involved, clear communication is both essential and more challenging. If this is you, this chapter will serve as a guide.

How to Have Difficult Discussions with Your Aging Parents

Each family has its own particular dynamics. In my everyday work, it's my job to identify these distinct details in order to provide solutions to my clients' financial problems. When it comes to estate planning, I've seen a wide range of behaviors. I've worked with parents who look forward to passing a financial legacy to their children and want to have open discussions regarding their assets. I've also seen greedy kids who can't wait to get their hands on a parent's estate. Whether raising the subject is second nature or wrought with tension, having frank conversations about a parent's estate raises delicate issues. Therefore, you must always approach the subject kindly and compassionately. The following are guidelines to follow:

Talk Plans, Not Net Worth

Many adult children are shocked when they learn that their moms and dads, who have always lived simply and frugally, have amassed incredible wealth. Most likely, their parents' modest lifestyles mean that they're reluctant to share information with their kids about their net worth. In this case, the last thing you want to ask is, "How much do you have, and who's getting it?" I recommend instead that you ask about their plans. For instance, get their feedback about the five fundamentals of an estate plan that I described in chapter 1: living trust, will, **advance medical directive**, power of attorney, and life insurance. Ask something such as, "Do you have any of these?"

Ask If They Will Owe Estate Tax

The answer to this estate tax question will provide you two important clues regarding their estate. First, if they're able to answer this question, it's a good sign that they have made plans beyond a simple will. Second, you'll have an idea of their net worth. If they say they'll owe estate taxes, you'll know that their net worth is at least higher than the exemption. As of 2011, the exemption is $5 million per person. This may change in the future. The bottom line is that if they know they have an estate tax problem, their net worth is in the multimillions.

Is the Surviving Parent Technically Savvy or Not?

My mother became very ill in 2010. I was the oldest of four sons, Dad had died more than a dozen years before, and Mom trusted my judgment. As a result, she fully disclosed information regarding her estate to me. I also took over as power of attorney and became her successor trustee. She was glad to delegate this responsibility because money management was not her skill or interest.

In many marriages, one spouse is the family CFO (Chief Financial Officer). Once the financially savvy spouse dies, the other often gladly passes the responsibility to trusted individuals—just as my mother did. If, on the other hand, the surviving parent has been the couple's money manager, he or she will be reluctant to hand over this role to you. In this case, get the basic facts about his or her estate plan. Then let your parent continue to manage the finances until he or she is no longer capable.

FEPA Is a Comprehensive Estate Planning Resource

Glenn Kautt, the president of our firm, conceived something we call a Formal Estate Plan Analysis, or **FEPA**, that I developed. It compiles all of the information I've shared so far, and also considers long-term care insurance, homeowner's insurance, and umbrella liability insurance. In addition, it calculates potential estate tax exposure. Finally, it addresses the beneficiaries of IRAs, 401(k)s or other retirement plans, life insurance, trusts, and other assets that have named beneficiaries. This final point—named beneficiaries—is critical. As I emphasized in chapter 1, any asset that has named beneficiaries *does not* pass via the will. In other words, an asset with a **beneficiary** will go directly to the beneficiary *regardless of what the will states.*

FEPA Ensures that Property Is Properly Titled

So what happens if the will states that one person will receive the asset but the joint tenant survivor is someone else? I worked with a couple who were both in their seventies. It was Bill and Jenny's second marriage. Jenny had a son with her first husband, while Bill and Jenny had three children together. Throughout their marriage Bill had managed the couple's finances. In both their wills, they stated that all assets would transfer to the surviving spouse, and then be equally divided among all four kids when the second spouse died.

Bill was later diagnosed with a serious heart condition. Jenny feared that if Bill died before her, she wouldn't know how to maintain her financial health. Therefore, she retitled their savings and **mutual fund** accounts to joint tenancy with Larry, her financially savvy son from her first marriage. Together the accounts were worth $750,000. But Bill did not die first; instead, Jenny was killed in a car accident. Larry instantly became legal owner of the savings and mutual fund accounts. Bill now found himself with no access to assets that he had once shared with Jenny. This put him in a difficult place because he needed to cover costly medical bills.

Improperly Titling Assets Can Tear a Family Apart

Jenny's death left Bill without money that was once his, and it also created complications within their family. Since Larry was sole owner of the mutual fund and savings account, Bill and Jenny's three children were legally entitled to none of the $750,000. Any amount they received was at Larry's discretion. Larry did his best to give part of his savings to his step-dad and his three half-siblings. Unfortunately the IRS considered these gifts that had adverse gift tax consequences for Larry. Despite their best efforts to maintain civility and fairness, the situation eroded the close relationship that Larry, his step-dad, and his three half-siblings once shared.

In another instance, I witnessed what happened when a wife died without changing the beneficiary from her ex-husband to her new spouse. Her rather large IRA wound up with the ex-husband. The new spouse's only recourse was to sue. Unfortunately this course of action not only was expensive but also proved useless in the end.

Do You Know Where Your Parents' Important Documents Are?

The FEPA also includes instructions that parents provide to their survivors. When a parent has a sudden medical emergency, the last thing you want is to have to scramble to find critical documents. This can lead to costly delays and add unnecessary stress to an already difficult situation. The following is a checklist of estate plan must-haves:

- Names and contact information of professional advisors such as CPAs, financial advisors, and insurance agents

- Names and addresses of former employers and employee ID numbers. These are important for pensions, insurance, retirement plans, and other benefits
- Contents of safe deposit boxes
- Location of estate documents, insurance policies, and current brokerage statements
- Location of prior years' tax returns
- Information about the primary residence and any other residences. These include settlement papers such as for HUD-1, deeds, a list of home improvements and their costs, and any appraisals. This will help to calculate cost basis if the house is sold prior to death.
- Bills and deposits that are set up for automatic payments
- Online accounts with user names, passwords, and ID numbers
- Any history of military service and eligibility for government benefits
- Information regarding prepaid funerals or burial plots
- List of mortgages, home equity lines of credit, and all debts (including credit cards), along with account numbers, balances, and payment due dates
- Money owed to them by other people

Use Holidays to Talk about Estate Planning

Major holidays, such as Thanksgiving, Christmas, and Rosh Hashanah, often bring families together. Therefore I recommend that parents take advantage of this time to review all beneficiary designations for their IRAs, 401(k)s, wills, trusts, and life insurance. If any of the beneficiaries have changed, parents can easily share this information with their children. As an adult child, the holidays are the perfect time to ask your parents about the basics of their estate plan. It will be easier to have this conversation if you carefully communicate to them that this is in their best interest. Imagine if illness, an accident, or any number of emergencies strikes them. Only when you fully comprehend their desires and plans are you able to make informed decisions on their behalf.

Ethical Wills Complement an Estate Plan

An ethical will is not a legal document. Instead it's a complement to an estate plan. It provides a way for parents to share personal values, beliefs, statements of faith, lessons, hopes, dreams, and other matters of intimate importance to family, friends, and community. An ethical will can become a cherished heirloom for the family. Therefore, it shouldn't contain negative or critical commentary. It should be written so as not to contradict or confuse other elements of the estate plan. An ethical will does not pass property to anyone. Rather it passes on matters of the heart and spirit. I provide clients examples of ethical wills as guides so they can compose their own for their family.

Schedule of Personal Property

You might think that money would cause the most intense fighting among heirs. Although that's often the case, you'd probably be surprised to hear that one of the most potentially problematic issues surrounding a parent's death is the distribution of personal effects such as jewelry, furniture, art, and even simple knickknacks. That's why I recommend that parents prepare a list of all their possessions. This detailed list is referred to as a schedule of personal property, and it's usually attached to the will rather than being directly part of it. In the time-consuming process of creating a comprehensive estate plan, many neglect to complete a schedule of personal property. Omitting this can lead to disputes that can stretch for years and may never be resolved.

To avoid conflict, it's best for parents to list their personal property and clearly designate who should receive what. This isn't something that you need to pay an estate planning attorney to do. Because it's a time-consuming process, hiring a lawyer to create one would probably be very expensive. One client took photos of her personal effects. She created envelopes for each of her children that contained images of the items that she intended each of them to receive.

As an adult child, focus on your parent's preparation of the personal property list, not on your desires. The appropriate question to ask while your parent is still alive and competent is *not*, "Who gets what?" or worse, "What am I getting?" Instead ask, "Have you prepared a list of your personal property and designated the person you want to receive each item?"

Having a parent die is one of the most difficult experiences you will ever endure. The combination of dealing with emotional loss and having to settle your parent's estate can lead to disputes among family members and unexpected expenses. Following the steps I've outlined in this chapter won't be easy, but the effort you and your parents put forth ahead of time will help you avoid potentially devastating situations. As much as you may be reluctant to have difficult estate planning conversations with your mom or dad, remember that most parents don't want their kids to hate one another and refuse to speak to each other due to a piece of jewelry or furniture. Therefore, planning ahead will instill confidence in you and your surviving parent. Both of you will know that everyone has done his or her best to leave a positive legacy for future generations.

In the next chapter, I'll describe what to expect after your parents die, and I'll show you how to work through the days and months after their passing.

Chapter 9

Softening the Blow

The bitterest tears shed over graves are for words
left unsaid and deeds left undone.
—Harriet Beecher Stowe

Ever since she could remember, Claudia was daddy's little girl. It didn't matter that decades had passed since her father had first told her those words—throughout her adulthood she maintained her position at the center of his life. Therefore, his death from a stroke at age seventy-five was the most emotionally painful moment she had ever experienced, and grieving her father's passing left her with little motivation to do much else. Her mother had died young, so Claudia was left with the task of settling the estate. So when she arrived at my office a week after he died, I knew that the last thing she wanted to do was to go through her father's paperwork and make seemingly countless calls to financial institutions.

Despite this, my client was financially savvy and knew that it was in her best interest to move forward, so she sought my help. Because Claudia's dad wasn't my client, however, my ability to help her was limited. In this chapter, I'll explain how I advised Claudia. Through her experience, you'll learn what to expect and what you need to do after a parent's death.

Document, Document, Document! And Make Sure Everyone Else Does the Same

When Claudia and I met, I had to give her a harsh dose of reality: taking charge of her dad's estate would require lots of phone calls, text messages, meetings, letter writing, filling out forms, envelope sealing, and e-mails.

In order to stay on top of the mountain of paperwork, I suggested that she create folders, physical and electronic, of all her correspondence. I advised her to take notes during important phone conversations and meetings and keep track of dates and times. Claudia had solid computer skills, so she could do this using her computer's e-mail, calendar, spreadsheet, and word processing applications. If she were computer-averse, I would have recommended that she write notes by hand and use a day planner to record correspondence dates. I also told Claudia to keep her father's will, trust, and the previous year's tax return nearby for quick reference and to make a copy of all letters.

"Cal, I'm overwhelmed with everything I'm supposed to do!" she confessed.

Having gone through my own dad's death, I knew exactly where she was coming from. After he died of a heart attack, I wasn't in the best mindset to take charge of critical estate planning matters. Like Claudia, I was the one who would have to bear most of this responsibility. Although my mother was still alive, my father had been the family money manager, which meant that my mom needed a lot of help wading through the morass of details.

"How about enlisting your siblings and friends to help you out?" I asked Claudia. I knew that my client had a younger brother and a tight-knit group of friends. "But make sure that they follow the same standards of record keeping that you do," I added.

Death Certificates and Burial or Cremation

In her father's will, he requested to be cremated. Unfortunately she realized that he had not made prepaid funeral arrangements. As a result, she had to cover the costs. She phoned me for my advice.

"I know that this is a tough time to make such an important decision. Unfortunately, prices can vary widely," I said. To make the process easier, I recommended that she talk to her minister or any friends she knew who had lost a loved one. She could ask them for recommendations of funeral homes that would compassionately explain her options and costs and not put any undue pressure on her.

While we were on the topic of funeral arrangements, I let her know that the funeral home would send the obituary to newspapers, file reports with authorities, and obtain copies of the death certificate for her. I told Claudia she needed at least twelve copies of a *certified* death certificate because each financial institution would require one to make changes to accounts and process claims.

If Your Parent Had a Financial Advisor, Contact Him or Her

One of the roles of a competent CFP® Professional is to provide survivors some guidance after his or her client's death. When Claudia contacted her dad's advisor, I suggested that she obtain the following:

- Brokerage account paperwork, which would allow her to access funds if the need arose
- **Net worth** statement, or at least a list of assets and liabilities, which would help her identify any potential challenges

If Claudia's dad didn't have a financial advisor, or if the advisor didn't provide these services, she would have to collect this information herself. This might be a simple or very complicated task based on her father's money management skills, her relationship with him, and his net worth. Remember, the higher a parent's net worth, the more complicated his or her estate will probably be.

How to Handle Bank Accounts and Insurance Companies

After Claudia's dad died, she didn't think that she could pay his bills with his checking account because it was titled to him alone. Fortunately her dad's accounts were in a trust, and she easily took over as successor trustee. Securing the accounts was as simple as providing a copy of the trust and death certificate to each financial institution. Once she did this, she had immediate access to all his accounts titled to the trust.

If you have joint accounts with your deceased parents, paying bills is as simple as writing checks as the joint tenant. However, keep in mind that there can be some gift tax and estate distribution problems as a result of this arrangement. In some states, joint bank accounts are automatically frozen upon the death of one of the joint owners. In the event that this happens, you'll have to wait until you file in **probate** court, and as the executor you will have to open a new checking account in the name of the estate. After this is established, you can write checks on the estate checking account in order to pay expenses and debts of the estate.

Again, I usually advise my clients to go the **revocable living trust** and power of attorney routes. This will avoid delays and complications.

As far as *life insurance* was concerned, Claudia was the sole **beneficiary** named in his policy. In order to receive death benefits, she had to provide written notification of her father's passing. This would require completing the insurance company's claim forms and submitting certified death certificates. I reminded her to keep copies of all correspondence.

What Not To Do

Claudia's dad had one checking account that was in his name only and not titled to the trust. In this case, where a checking account is not titled jointly or in a trust, the survivor's hands are tied. According to state law in virtually every state, when an account is titled only to the individual who died (in this case, Claudia's dad alone), his estate immediately becomes the owner—the account cannot be used until someone is appointed by the court to administer the estate (if the deceased person had a will, the court would appoint the executor named in the will). In fact, the account is technically off limits until the estate is settled (in other words, after the probate process is completely finished). In the meantime, a judge may issue a letter to allow the executor or estate administrator to write checks on the account but only to pay costs of the estate. Family members and other likely heirs should resist the temptation to forge the deceased's name on checks to pay bills or use the deceased's ATM or debit card to obtain cash. Forgery is fraud, as is any other unauthorized access to someone's bank account. Forging a check, even if you are the heir, is a big no-no.

The rules may sound strict, but they exist for a very good reason—it's important that the appropriate person handle the estate administration legally. Sometimes an heir wants to move quickly, but at the same time, it is critical to preserve the estate so it is dealt with in accordance with state law and to fulfill the deceased person's desires. Don't do something stupid and get yourself or the family in trouble because someone needs cash and they're in a rush to get the money. It's just not worth the risk.

Contacting Social Security

"I have a check from Social Security payable to my dad. What do I do with this?" Claudia asked me. I told her that she needed to contact Social Security immediately and inform them of her father's passing so that they would cease benefits. The last thing she wanted was for the government to demand payment for several months of Social Security checks that she had already cashed but were not hers to begin with.

Contacting Creditors and Employers

Claudia wrote letters to her father's creditors and credit card companies informing them of his death. Her dad had mortgage life insurance and a life insurance policy that covered his car loan. In some cases, these policies directly pay off the balances due. In other cases, the insurance company sends a check payable to the beneficiary. If you are the beneficiary and receive a check, you can decide whether to pay off the debts or invest the money.

I suggested that Claudia write formal letters to her dad's employer, trade union, or any other group or professional organization that he was associated with. He might have had insurance policies with these institutions and Claudia might be a beneficiary.

When Do I Contact a Lawyer?

Claudia's dad lived in Virginia and also owned property in Texas. Possessing property in another state usually results in what's called ancillary probate. Again, one of the advantages of **titling** out-of-state property to a revocable living trust is to avoid ancillary probate. Because this was not done by her father, it meant that Claudia would have to go through probate in both Virginia *and* Texas. I recommended that she find a lawyer in Texas who, for a reasonable fee, handled probate. When she met with him or her, she needed to clearly communicate about costs before cutting the lawyer a check. I also recommended that she prepare ahead of time by bringing a checklist of questions that she needed answered.

"But my cousin lives in Texas, owns a home there, and told me exactly what I needed to do," Claudia told me.

"Friends and family are there to support you during difficult times. Unfortunately their advice is no substitute for an expert," I said. I explained that estates, particularly high net worth ones, were complex. Well-intended recommendations could serve as a starting point, but because probate could be simple or complicated—depending on the state, the type of property, and the value—she should *never* take suggestions from nonprofessionals as the final authority.

Take the Slow and Steady Approach to Settling Your Parent's Estate

If you rush through the intricacies of resolving an estate, you risk making mistakes that could cost you considerable money and time. I've seen clients lose thousands of dollars in taxes that could otherwise have been avoided, and I've witnessed banks freeze their parents' accounts, which has created misery for cash-strapped clients.

At the same time, procrastinating can lead to its own set of problems. For instance, federal law requires that an estate tax return be filed within nine months of the death, although an extension filed in a timely manner can give you an extra six months. Tax laws constantly change, so be sure to seek expert advice from CFP® Professionals, CPAs, and lawyers. They'll help you determine your full tax liability. In addition, if a wealthy heir is going to disclaim assets for his or her own estate planning purposes, a qualified written disclaimer must be delivered to the executor or trustee within nine months of the date of death.

Speaking of taxes, there are four different returns that may have to be filed after your last parent dies:

1. Final 1040 income tax return.

2. Form 1041 estate income tax return for any investment income of assets that are still in probate. You must obtain a federal tax ID number for the estate and put this on the estate income tax return. Don't confuse this with an estate tax return (Form 706—see number 4 below). The 1041 is for tax on *income* to the estate; the 706 is a tax levied on the value of the *assets* of the estate.

3. A trust income tax return, which is also Form 1041. This is for income derived from assets that were in a revocable living trust, which becomes irrevocable upon death. You must obtain a new federal tax ID number for the **irrevocable trust** and put it on the trust tax return. Also, the accounts in the revocable trust will need to be retitled to the irrevocable trust account.

4. Form 706, which is an estate tax return. You need this if the estate exceeded the exclusion amount, currently $5 million. Your state may also have an estate (or inheritance) tax return that must be filed. For example, Maryland imposes an estate tax while Virginia doesn't.

Initially, Claudia sought to settle her dad's estate as soon as possible. I advised her to slow down, particularly in regard to distributing property and money to beneficiaries. Let's say that in a rush to sort out her father's estate, she handed out all assets to his beneficiaries as quickly as she could. She later discovered a debt that had not been paid off or a tax bill that was due. As executor, she would be held personally responsible for this and would have to pay for it with her own money. To avoid this scenario, I told her to first pay all debts and other expenses, and then distribute a small amount to the beneficiaries. I advised her that she should keep quite a bit of cash in reserve until after all the tax returns had been filed. Once she had done her best to make sure all possible costs or claims of creditors were taken care of, then and only then should she fully distribute the estate.

Tracking Cost Basis

Cost basis in its simplest form is what you paid for an asset. For instance, if you bought stock at $100 per share, the $100 is the cost basis. It is important to know the cost basis in order to correctly calculate a **capital gain.** That way you'll pay the appropriate tax on that gain (in tax parlance, gain means profit). The formula to calculate capital gain is as follows:

Net proceeds – the adjusted cost basis = capital gain

It's not always that simple, however, to calculate cost basis. In the case of **mutual funds** that reinvest dividends and capital gains distributions or for stocks that have Dividend Reinvestment Plans (DRIPs), the dividends, capital gains, or both are added to the cost basis because you already paid tax on those items each year. In addition, if you own a rental property, you are entitled to deduct depreciation each year, but the cost basis decreases every year in the amount of the depreciation. That's why the word "adjusted" appears in the capital gain formula above. Tracking cost basis is extremely important because whenever an investment or other asset, such as a house, is sold, you must pay capital gains tax on the profit. As you can see, tracking cost basis can be simple or complex, so it's always best to keep good records and consult with a tax expert.

Probate

Claudia had heard plenty of probate nightmare stories, and she was scared of the process. No doubt it can be a thorny matter, and one that can be even more complicated if the estate is large, the probatable assets are extensive, and there are claims against it. I first recommended that she contact the county probate court for instructions. In her state there was a **de minimus** amount that allowed for a simplified probate process. Because of her father's high net worth, I advised her to work with an attorney. I reminded her that the following were *not* probatable assets:

- Insurance policies
- IRAs, 401(k)s, and other qualified retirement accounts
- Jointly owned accounts or property
- Anything titled to a trust

Even if she were certain that there would be very little to probate because nearly all her dad's assets were in a trust, retirement accounts, and joint accounts, I still advised her to slowly distribute assets. She might owe federal taxes, state taxes, or both, and she needed to be sure that there was enough liquidity in the trust to cover costs.

401(k)s, IRAs, and Other Qualified Retirement Accounts

Claudia had two options when it came to her dad's retirement accounts:

1. Take the money in a lump sum and pay income tax on the entire amount immediately. I warned her that this was usually not a good idea because the tax hit is immediate and could throw her into a much higher tax bracket; that is, she might go from a 25 percent marginal

tax rate to a 35 percent rate. So the federal tax on a $1 million IRA would be $350,000!

2. Stretch out payments over her life expectancy and pay annual income tax on the smaller amount. Each year she would receive a small distribution, based on an IRA table that factored in her remaining life expectancy; she would only have to pay tax on the amount distributed each year. In addition, the amount remaining in the inherited IRA would continue to grow tax deferred. In this case, the retirement account should remain in the name of the deceased and FBO (For the Benefit Of) the beneficiary. This option would save her and her surviving relatives hundreds of thousands of dollars over their lifetimes. She would also have the option of withdrawing more than the required minimum if she needed to.

Home Appraisals and Brokerage Accounts After Death

Whenever a client dies, I recommend that his or her heirs contact a real estate agent and have the agent provide a written estimate of the current market value of the house. In some cases, a formal appraisal may be required, but these are typically much more expensive to do. Determining the market value is important because the house will get what's referred to as "stepped up basis," which means that it will be appraised at **fair market value** as of the date of the death. The result is little to no capital gains tax if the heirs decide to sell the house. For example, let's say your parents paid $100,000 for their house forty years ago, and upon their death it's worth $500,000. If you sell it a few months after their passing, your capital gain would *not* be $400,000 ($500,000 minus $100,000). Instead, the capital gain would be $0 ($500,000 minus $500,000) because the home's basis gets stepped up to $500,000, which was the fair market value at death.

All investments in brokerage accounts such as stocks, bonds, and mutual funds also receive a step-up in basis. When Claudia asked her father's financial advisor about this, she could tell that he didn't really understand the process. She voiced her concern to me, and I warned her that neglecting to address this correctly could result in a very expensive mistake. If you do not understand the "step-up" process, and your parents' broker doesn't seem to either, you should run, not walk, to a financial advisor who does understand these issues.

Disposing of Personal Property

Claudia had followed my advice, and as a result she was able to settle her father's estate with as little heartache and struggle as possible. First, she had paid off all debts and taxes before distributing her father's assets to beneficiaries. Then she shredded boxes of documents that her dad had saved over the years. She had also thrown away many of his unclaimed possessions. By this point, most of his belongings were gone. Some items remained, which she knew that she could sell. One of her friends regularly posted items on Craigslist and eBay, and she enlisted his help. Through his guidance, she learned the value of taking multiple, high-quality photos of auction items; how to competitively price them; and how to compose short yet informative descriptions.

As the saying goes, "Time heals all wounds." Claudia and I worked closely together, and as the emotional pain diminished, the fond memories increased. No doubt losing her dad was heart-wrenching. But for the most part, he had planned his estate well, which allowed her to avoid painful pitfalls. If, on the other hand, he had added the burden of a poorly planned estate to her already vulnerable emotional state, the situation could have been unbearable. In my experience of consulting many grieving individuals, I've seen estate planning at both its best and worst. In the end, I'm convinced that proper estate planning is a gesture of love.

In the next chapter, you'll learn how to prevent the potentially devastating consequences of identity theft. I'll also provide steps to take when you've become a victim of identity fraud.

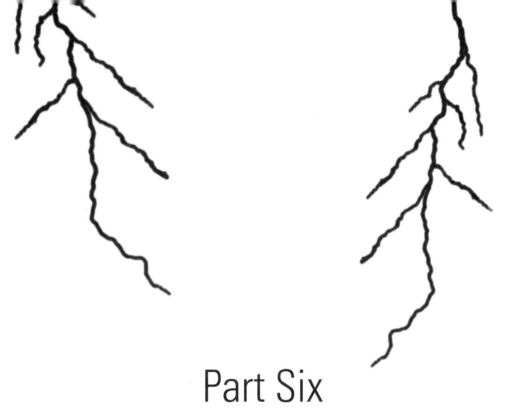

Part Six

What If I Lost My Identity?

Chapter 10

Taking Measures, Taking Charge

*I don't need to worry about identity theft
because no one wants to be me.*
—comedian Jay London

Planning Ahead

If you had warned me thirty years ago of the dangers of identity theft, I would have told you to stop watching so many sci-fi films. After all, most of the weapons of mass identity fraud weren't part of daily life back then. Recall in chapter 5 that I mentioned a number of yesterday's technological novelties that have become today's essential tools. Unfortunately the unprecedented advances also have disadvantages. The lightning speed of information flow means that our digital identities go along for the ride, winding their way—quite literally—around the world. The result is that identity theft has become the fastest growing crime in the United States. In 2009, the Federal Trade Commission (FTC), reported millions of victims of Internet-driven fraud.

In part one of this chapter, I'll provide you measures to take in order to avoid falling prey to this criminal epidemic. In part two, I'll guide you through the essential steps that you need to follow in the event that your identity has been stolen. If you're a self-professed nontechie, you're in good company. In fact, there are two statements my colleagues hear me say all the time: "Technology is great . . . when it works" and "Doing things on the computer is really easy . . . if you know how." So rest assured that this guide will be free of technical jargon.

What Is Identity Theft?

The Identity Theft Resource Center (www.idtheftcenter.org), which is a nonprofit group, subdivides identity fraud into the following five categories:

1. **Business and commercial**: Using another business's name to obtain credit
2. **Criminal:** Posing as another person when caught for a crime
3. **Financial:** Using another person's identity to obtain credit, goods, and services
4. **Cloning:** Stealing another person's information in order to assume his or her identity in daily life. This could be for praise or attention, or to hide from law enforcement, creditors, or immigration officials.
5. **Medical:** obtaining medical care, drugs, or even reimbursement from health insurance claims

In this chapter, we will focus primarily on number 3, financial, because this is the most widespread form of identity theft. With that said, many of the concepts that I'll cover will apply to the other categories as well.

Review Credit Reports

The first step to protecting yourself is to obtain copies of your credit report from all three major credit reporting agencies: Equifax, TransUnion, and Experian. At www.annualcreditreport.com, you can get one free report per year. In addition, each of the credit bureaus offers services that will charge you a fee to monitor your credit and report all activities, both suspicious and valid. You can also pay for a "credit lock" service, which prevents or limits inquiries into your credit reports. This is important because excessive credit inquiries can lower your credit score. As a consequence, it may be more difficult to obtain a loan or you may be charged a higher interest rate.

Be careful of free credit report advertisements that appear online, in print, and on TV and radio. Most of these aren't really free because you have to sign up for a monthly service in order to receive the so-called free benefit. With that said, enrolling in one of them may be worthwhile. Other types of credit monitoring services that are up-front about their fees include LifeLock, Guard Dog, Identity Guard, and TrustedID. These are third-party companies that provide legitimate services. In 2010, LifeLock lost a lawsuit that accused it of deceptive advertising practices (although it did not claim the company's services were not good). Despite this, many people have had good experiences with the company. Whether you obtain reports for a fee or free of charge, review them carefully for errors and suspicious activities. If you see anything odd, contact the credit agencies right away and resolve any possible conflicts. The following are the web addresses where you can file a dispute claim:

- **Equifax:** www.ai.equifax.com/CreditInvestigation
- **TransUnion:** www.transunion.com/corporate/personal/creditDisputes/submitDispute.page

- **Experian:** www.experian.com/disputes/disputes.html

With all your options, which service should you sign up for? The saying "You get what you pay for" is worth considering in this case. While you can receive a degree of protection free of charge, you should expect to pay for comprehensive support. When clients ask me whether they should enroll in a credit monitoring service, I start by asking them if it's a top concern. If their answer is yes, I tell them that paying a monthly fee may be worth the peace of mind.

Guard Your Social Security Number and Date of Birth

Once Internet connectivity reached critical mass, Social Security numbers suddenly became our default personal IDs. Then we realized that crooks armed with our date of birth in one hand and our Social Security number in the other could deal a deadly blow to our financial security.

Criminals who have both your Social Security number and birth date can open multiple credit cards in your name and immediately max out their limits. Some will even file income taxes using your identity; then they'll line their pockets with refunds that are based on falsified tax information. Unfortunately it may take years for you to even discover the fraud because the IRS and the state taxing authority will send notices to the address that the thief set up. The moment you do find out that someone has filed tax returns in your name, you must submit a completed IRS Form 8822 to formally change your address to the correct one.

Use a Paper Shredder

My wife once witnessed two guys stealing neighborhood trash. They pulled up to the residences, grabbed garbage bags from the bins, and tossed the bags into the bed of their rental truck. My wife immediately called the police and gave them the location, description. and license plate number of the truck. The homeowners who had shredded their documents were safe, but those who hadn't bothered to shred probably had bags stuffed with preapproved credit card applications, mortgage solicitations, and blank checks issued by their credit card companies—a swindler's dream!

Phone and E-mail Scams

Phishing is the practice of sending fraudulent e-mails that appear as if they are from credible sources. The goal is to steal your personal information. For instance, you may receive an e-mail that appears to be from your credit card company. The "American Express" or "Chase" logo may show up in the message and the e-mail address in the "from" field may even say "amex. com" or "chase.com."

You read the message and it tells you that the financial institution has noticed unauthorized activity on your account. They are now requiring you to log on to their official site in order to confirm your purchases. Unfortunately the message warning you of fraud is itself a fraudulent message.

The e-mail will have a link directing you to a website that may look just like your financial institution's. Once you click on that link and input your username and password, you've given the criminals enough information to steal your identity.

One simple way to avoid being caught in a phishing scam is to thoroughly read any e-mail message that appears to be from your financial institution. Then open your web browser and use the web address you've used in the past to log in to your financial institution's website. *Do not* click on the link that's provided in the e-mail itself. Once you've signed in, you'll see if you've received any legitimate messages from the bank or credit card company.

If e-mails from any government agency arrive in your inbox, such as the Social Security Administration, the IRS, or your state taxing authority, never accept these as legitimate. The government sends notices to you only through the US Postal Service and never via e-mails or text messages.

If any e-mail—financial or otherwise—is suspicious, my rule of thumb is to delete it. If you don't know the sender, get rid of the message. If it's important and legitimate, the person or organization will find a way to get in touch with you. You're under no legal, social, or moral obligation to open e-mails.

Phishing scams aren't limited to computers. A text message purporting to be from your financial institution may appear on your mobile device. According to the message, the bank claims it needs to verify purchases you've made, and it's asking you to give them a call. Confirm that the phone number matches the actual company's contact information before you make the call.

When it comes to your phone lines, both wireless and wired, make sure you've entered your numbers on the "National Do Not Call Registry" at either www.donotcall.gov or 1-888-382-1222. This is a free service. Even after you've done this, you'll probably still receive phone solicitations. The sales reps on the other end of the phone can be very persuasive and sound like they're contacting you from legitimate organizations. Be sure that you *never* provide a telemarketer your Social Security number, credit card number, or other essential bits of personal information.

Monitor Your Bills

Not only do you need to do a line-by-line review of monthly account summaries that you receive from credit card companies, banks, and brokerages, you also need to make sure you receive statements every month. If one doesn't show up in the mail, it may mean that someone has diverted your letters to another address. By the time you realize this has happened, a criminal may have already amassed an identity-crushing amount of information about you. If you have opted to go "paperless" by only receiving statements online, you should log in and check your statements every month for erroneous charges.

Identity Theft Insurance

Identity theft insurance is worth considering, particularly if you have a high **net worth** estate to protect. Not all property and casualty insurance companies offer this type of protection, so you may have to find a policy on your own if your insurance broker doesn't provide this option. When clients have asked me for help, I've put them in touch with independent agents who provide fraud insurance.

Computer Safety

You should *never* access the Internet unless you've installed antivirus software. The two big players in computer protection are McAfee and Norton, although there are other fine companies as well. If you're uncertain which product to purchase, consider seeking recommendations from friends and colleagues who have solid computer knowledge. I've also found that computer-savvy sons and daughters can be great resources as well. In addition, CNET provides reviews of antivirus software (www.cnet.com).

When a trusted site asks for payment or other personal information, make sure that it is secure. There are two basic security features to look out for. First, at the top of your web browser where you input the web address (also called the URL), check to see if there is an "s" after the "http." It should read "https." This tells you that your data is being encrypted and delivered to a secure site. Second, some web browsers, such as Microsoft Internet Explorer, show a tiny padlock icon in the lower-right corner of the browser window that indicates that the site has taken security precautions. In addition, some antivirus software programs will let you know whether or not a site is safe. If you're using a wireless router, make sure that it's password protected. Allowing anyone to access your wireless network will not only slow down your connection but also will put you at risk.

When you're away from home, be careful about using the Internet. Avoid logging onto accounts on public computers, such as those in libraries and Internet cafes. Although Wi-Fi hotspots in airports, coffeehouses, and retail stores make it easy to open your laptop and hop online, avoid using public Wi-Fi to access personal accounts such as banks, health care, and e-commerce. Unscrupulous techies have devices that can intercept the connection between your computer and the Wi-Fi source. Some go as far as to create hotspots that lure unsuspecting web surfers.

Maintain a List of Key Account Information and Guard It Closely

Protecting your identity is like a game of "Whac-A-Mole." In this amusement park diversion, you use a mallet to hammer down every toy mole that pops up; the moment you successfully hammer one into its hole, another emerges. In the identity fraud version of "Whac-A-Mole," I suggest that you first record all of your financial accounts, including account numbers, phone numbers, and passwords, on a single spreadsheet.

Now you've successfully put one mole back in its hole. Unfortunately this same document is the pot of gold at the end of a swindler's rainbow. If you save the spreadsheet in a place that makes it accessible when you need it most, say in a laptop computer or smart phone, you've increased the risk to your electronic devices. One way to guard this spreadsheet is to password-protect it, but then you must safeguard the password and make sure that a few loved ones who need to know about it keep it secure as well. My point is that in our complex society, every time you come up with a solution, another problem emerges.

Guard PINs and Credit Cards

Who should know your passwords and Personal Identification Numbers (PINs)? I recommend that you limit this to your spouse and one adult child who is mature enough to handle this enormous responsibility. If you have multiple credit cards (something that I usually advise against), don't carry all of them with you. Only take the cards that you'll need on a daily basis. When it comes to passwords that you use for online accounts, generate ones that are difficult to guess. Strong passwords include a mix of numbers, symbols, and both uppercase and lowercase letters. *Never* use your date of birth or address. Also consider changing your passwords regularly.

Technological advances in payment methods have made it more convenient than ever to make purchases, but this convenience has also increased risk. For instance, there are credit cards and mobile phones that don't require a signature or swipe. Wave one of these cards or your electronic device in front of a payment terminal and your purchase is processed instantly. Imagine if someone gets a hold of one of these advanced credit cards or your mobile phone linked to your credit account. The crook can easily spend your hard-earned money before you even know you've lost your payment device. Rather than be an early adopter, I've maintained a conservative stance with these innovations. Therefore I've decided to wait before making the next generation of payment part of my daily life.

While I'm on the topic of mobile devices, now that phones are more mini-computers than telephones, be aware that they have become susceptible to viruses and malware. Phones that have Bluetooth enabled at all times are at risk, so consider switching off Bluetooth when you're not using it. This will also increase your battery life.

Credit cards are much safer than debit cards. If a fraudulent charge appears on your credit card statement, you can dispute it and the credit card company will reimburse you for the amount charged up to a certain limit. However, a debit card provides direct access to the cash in your checking account, and if that cash is stolen it is gone. You have no recourse. So if you have a choice, always use credit cards instead of debit cards.

Social Networking

Facebook, LinkedIn, Myspace, and other social networking sites have spread our personal information around the world. Criminals have used these sites to find details about members. They have successfully accessed Social Security numbers, dates of birth, phone numbers, addresses, and more through the content that subscribers have posted. The following are a few ways to safeguard yourself against cyber delinquents:

- Avoid posting your year of birth online.
- Carefully review privacy settings on sites such as Facebook, and consider making your content viewable to a limited audience.

- Do not post updates regarding where you are located at any given time. Whether it's an evening out with friends or a weekend in a faraway destination, save the sharing of photos and comments until *after* you've returned home.
- Think carefully about personal information you post such as photos, facts about you, your likes and dislikes, and more. Your social networking habits may make it easy for crooks to steal your identity.

If you think that your personal information will be of no interest to anyone or that it's difficult to get a hold of, I suggest you do a Google search using your name. You may be unpleasantly surprised at what information circulates about you in cyberspace.

Prepare Ahead Before You Travel Abroad

You should contact your credit card companies before your trip and let them know when you'll be away. Be sure to write down the toll-free customer service number of each card that you're planning to carry, and keep this information separate from your wallet. After all, this precautionary action will do you no good if you've stored the information in a wallet that's been stolen.

A few years ago, my wife and I took a trip to Russia. We were with our tour group visiting a Russian Orthodox Church. It was in that sacred place where one of our group members was pickpocketed. Fortunately her credit card company was the same as mine, so we called the international phone number on the back of my card to immediately block her account. As a result, no fraudulent charges appeared on her credit card.

Restaurants Put Your Identity at Risk

Once you receive your bill at a restaurant, you typically hand your credit card to the server. At this point, you've put your financial information in their hands. While the vast majority of waitstaff are ethical, some are not. In either case, servers can do whatever they want with your credit card. Aside from following them to the register, watching them swipe your card, and taking it back immediately, there's not much you can do. What you can do is make sure you take all receipts with you.

As a young adult, my son worked as a waiter. Because of his experience, he advised me to always take my copy of the credit card receipt and the original bill for the meal as well. He told me that dishonest waiters could commit fraud by using the financial information that diners left behind; at minimum, they could increase the tip on the signed receipt.

Dealing with Reality

As a CFP® Professional, part of my everyday work is to encourage my clients to take charge of their finances as soon as possible. They don't always heed my advice, and as a result they suffer the consequences. In the event of identity theft, procrastination could be fatal to your financial life. Quick action, on the other hand, could stop thieves from doing even more damage than they may have already done.

For example, one of my clients realized that his identity had been stolen once he saw significant out-of-state charges on his monthly credit card statement. As a result, Stan took the following steps:

1. He contacted the police and reported the fraudulent charges. They provided him a case number.

2. He contacted his credit card company and informed them of the unauthorized charges. They canceled the card, issued him a new one, and removed the charges from his account.

3. He filed the fraud with the Federal Trade Commission.

4. He contacted the three credit bureaus and enrolled his credit cards for credit watch, and they monitored his activity for over a year.

Stan's quick action combined with the straightforward nature of the crime committed against him resulted in an identity theft case that was resolved quickly with just a little effort on his part. In severe cases, sorting out identity fraud will take time—perhaps years—and a great deal of effort, such as making countless phone calls, keeping track of written correspondence, and filling out forms. Your situation may be as easy to fix as Stan's, or it may require unraveling events as complicated as any on TV's *CSI*. The truth is there are probably just as many different identity fraud scenarios as there are criminals themselves. This also means that there is no one-size-fits-all formula for resolving the situation.

With that said, the primary steps to take after finding out that your identity has been stolen are the same for everyone. If you believe that you've become a victim of fraud, immediately notify the following:

- The police
- All three credit reporting bureaus
- Your bank(s)
- The US Federal Trade Commission, where you'll complete the ID Theft Affidavit: ftc.gov/bcp/edu/resources/forms/affidavit.pdf

- Your credit card companies
- Your investment accounts and your financial advisor

You can essentially "lock down" your credit card by purchasing a service from one of the credit bureaus. Once you enroll, you'll be able to set your account preferences for access.

You may have to close accounts with your financial institutions and open new ones. You should ask your bank and credit card companies about the extent of your liabilities. In many cases, your liability will be zero, but you should make sure. Once you've shut down your accounts, don't forget to update your account information with any companies, utilities, or organizations that automatically charge your credit card or withdraw from your checking accounts. Otherwise, you may have to pay penalties for unpaid bills. If you've purchased identity theft insurance, you should immediately notify the agent from whom you bought the coverage and complete the appropriate paperwork.

In the next chapter, we'll address how to remain in solid financial shape despite possible declines in your health.

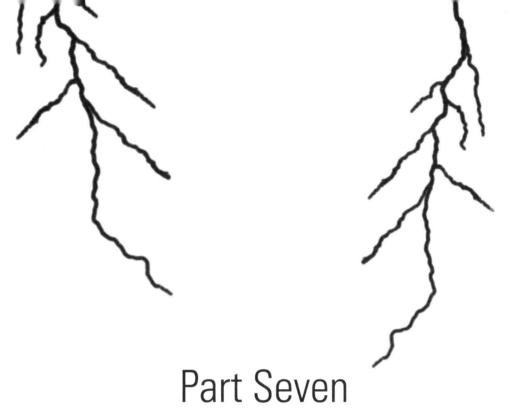

Part Seven

What If I Lost My Health?

Chapter 11

Accepting the Two *Ms*

Look to your health; and if you have it, praise God and value it next to conscience; for health is the second blessing that we mortals are capable of, a blessing money can't buy.
—Izaak Walton (1593–1683)

If we live long enough, most of us will have to deal with health problems—and in many instances, they'll be major ones. In my case, I had triple heart bypass surgery at forty-five years of age. A few years later, my wife had a double bypass. Talk about estate planning wake-up calls! As we grow older, all of us will become keenly aware of the two Ms: mortality and morbidity. We grow to accept death and disease as an inevitable part of the aging process. When it comes to protecting our loved ones and ourselves, health insurance is the first planning solution that comes to mind.

Unless you haven't been paying attention, you know that major health-care legislation was passed in 2010. Although the health-care bill became law, many of its provisions won't take effect until 2013. In the meantime, many states have filed lawsuits over certain aspects of medical insurance reform. Time will tell what the final result will look like. In this chapter, I'll provide an overview of the health insurance basics that will most likely remain relevant regardless of changes within our nation's system.

Your Options

First, a pithy piece of profound wisdom: Whatever your health insurance is, make sure it's good. This may not seem like life-altering advice, but allow me to explain. "Good" means different things to different people. For instance, many have become accustomed to insurance that requires a minimal cash outlay for them. That's good if you can get it, but because of rising health-care costs, many businesses and individuals are opting for high-deductible plans since they charge less up-front; in other words, the monthly premiums are lower. In exchange, you have to pay more of the initial costs until you reach your deductible amount. No one likes paying high deductibles, but if you shift your view of health insurance and think of it as taking care of big expenses, such as catastrophic illnesses or injuries that could potentially wipe out your savings, then this is good coverage. Meanwhile, you'll be responsible for paying for the smaller stuff.

In addition to basic health coverage, there are three supplemental insurance products that you should consider:

- **Medicare** supplemental health insurance (Medigap)
- **Disability income insurance** (DII)
- Long-term care insurance (LTCI)

Medicare versus Medicaid

If you're a US citizen, Medicare becomes your primary health insurance once you celebrate your sixty-fifth birthday. This is not to be mistaken for the similar-sounding "**Medicaid**," which is a poverty program. Within Medicare, there are several options, and you should become familiar with their costs and coverage, and especially with the costs and coverage associated with prescription drugs. The intricacies of Medicare choices are beyond the scope of this book, but you can conduct additional research online at www.medicare.gov, which is the official US website for Medicare. You can also find information on www.goodcare.com, the website of a friend of mine, Dr. Katy Votava.

Because Medicare doesn't pay for everything, I highly recommend that you obtain supplemental coverage to fill in the gaps. This type of insurance is called Medigap, and many employers offer it. If your employer doesn't have this, you should research the coverage and premiums sold by insurance companies and groups such as AARP (formerly known as American Association of Retired Persons).

The relatively new Medicare Part C, also known as the "Medicare Advantage Plan," has been receiving positive reviews from experts in the field. If you are approaching your sixty-fifth birthday, you should definitely look into it and consider purchasing it.

Disability Income Insurance (DII)

This may come as a surprise to you, but in many instances financial advisors believe that disability income insurance is more important than health insurance. The reason is that if you're under age sixty-five and still working, the loss of your income due to long-term disability from major illnesses or injuries could be more financially devastating than a major surgery. For instance, let's say that a major surgery costs $75,000. If your income is $100,000 per year, and you become disabled at forty-five years of age and are unable to ever work again, the loss is a staggering $2 million (20 years x $100,000 = $2 million; the 20 reflects that it will take two decades until you become sixty-five years old). That figure doesn't even factor in raises you would probably get in those twenty years of working. Compare $2 million of lost income to the $75,000 cost of major surgery.

Many employers provide group disability insurance at little to no cost to the employee. Typically this insurance will cover 60 percent of your salary, but it has a cap of $5,000 per month, which translates to $60,000 per year (12 months x $5,000). Thus if your income exceeds $100,000 per year, your disability benefit will be less than 60 percent of your salary. In this case, you should strongly consider purchasing additional individual DII to reach a combined total of 60 percent of your salary.

If your employer pays the premium, and you become disabled and qualify for benefits, you're responsible for the taxes on the monthly income that you receive from the policy. If you pay the premium yourself, however, the disability income insurance benefits are income-tax free. One of the major roadblocks to enrolling in DII is that it's often difficult to qualify for. When insurance companies conduct the underwriting, they not only assess your health but also your occupation. Another difficulty is that individual policies are much more expensive than group ones. Despite the high prices, if tragedy strikes you'll be glad you're covered.

Two Long-Term Care Insurance (LTCI) Options

"Cal, should I buy long-term care insurance?" ranks among the top ten most frequently asked questions that I receive from clients. My answer is always the same: "It depends."

In major metropolitan areas, nursing home costs and home health costs can easily run from $80,000 to $100,000 per year and even more. Meanwhile, LTCI premiums may run from $2,000 to $5,000 per year. (The amount is based on your age, health condition, and the amount of monthly benefits you desire, as well as other factors.) So unless your **net worth** is in the millions of dollars, you should buy LTCI. Why?

Let's say that your assets are less than $1 million. A $100,000 annual nursing home bill would wipe out your nest egg in ten years or less—not a very long time considering that people can live decades with major illnesses. I've worked with couples who, despite my recommendation, decided to not purchase long-term care insurance. Suddenly, a husband or wife is diagnosed with Alzheimer's disease. The disease progresses and leaves the spouse physically and mentally incapacitated. Exorbitant long-term care costs wipe out the couple's assets, and they find themselves in poverty and have to apply for Medicaid. LTCI is not cheap, but the benefits of investing in it far exceed the costs of living your final years in abject misery.

The premiums that you pay for LTCI are tax deductible as medical expenses, but there is a 7.5 percent *Adjusted Gross Income* (AGI) threshold that you must meet before you can deduct expenses. So in

> Adjusted Gross Income is your total income before deductions. It's line 37 on the 2010 Form 1040 tax return.

reality, you may not be able to deduct the premiums if you're a high-income earner. Unlike DII, one major advantage of LTCI is that the benefits you receive from it are tax-free—even if your employer paid the premium.

The better LTCI policies will pay for in-home care as well as nursing home costs, but they don't cover everything. For example, if you move into an assisted living facility that doesn't include nurses who will monitor your health and administer your prescription medications, LTCI will most likely not pay your monthly rent. It's key that you clearly understand what the insurance will and will not cover. The policies usually explain these in terms of six Activities of Daily Living (ADLs):

- Eating (feeding yourself)
- Personal hygiene and grooming
- Dressing and undressing
- Toileting
- Ambulation (walking and moving around)
- Functional transfers (getting out of bed)

Typically an LTCI policy will pay benefits when you are unable to perform two or more of these ADLs.

If, on the other hand, your net worth is high enough, you may be better off self-insuring; in other words, instead of buying LTCI, you would use your income and investment assets to cover the nursing home expenses yourself. Imagine that you have $4 million in assets and that a nursing home costs $100,000 per year. If you combined your Social Security ($2,000 per month equals $24,000 per year) and pension income ($4,000 per month equals $48,000 per year) and you withdrew 5 percent of your investment assets ($4 million x 5% equals $200,000 per year), you could easily meet your monthly nursing home costs without LTCI. In this scenario, your kids would inherit less. You would also save $2,000 to $5,000 per year in insurance costs, however, which would add to their inheritance.

When high net worth clients aren't sure what to do, I tell them, "Because this is an estate planning issue, and not one about whether you'll have enough income to survive, the question now becomes, how much do you want your kids to inherit?" Once they determine their course of action, I recommend that they clearly inform their families of the reasons behind their decision.

Who Qualifies for DII and LTCI?

With these types of insurance, I always tell my clients, "You have to prove you don't need it in order to get it." This means that once you have a major health problem, it may be difficult at best, impossible at worst, to enroll. That's why it's usually easier and less expensive to qualify for DII and LTCI when you're younger and in good health.

With that said, if you've had some health issue in the past, this doesn't rule out DII and LTCI outright. To be certain, talk to a knowledgeable insurance agent or simply apply for coverage. You may discover that your preexisting condition may not disqualify you, but you may be "rated," which means that you will be issued a policy at a higher cost. You may be afraid that if you apply and are approved that you must enroll. Don't worry; if you decide later that you don't want to spend the money, you aren't obligated to buy the policy.

Two Fundamental Terms about DII and LTCI

The waiting period refers to the length of time you agree to wait before benefits kick in after illness strikes. For example, you could decide to wait from three to six months or even a year. The longer the waiting period, the less expensive the premium will be. When you're sick or out of work, you could quickly amass substantial bills within weeks, let alone months, so consider the waiting period carefully.

The benefit period is how long the insurance company will pay benefits. For DII, it could be until you reach sixty-five years of age or for your entire life. The longer the benefit period, the higher the premium will be. For LTCI, coverage could be any specific number of years or for a lifetime.

There are many more technical issues regarding Medigap, DII, and LTCI. An insurance expert should be able to patiently and clearly answer your questions until you fully understand the coverage and costs. In the next chapter, you'll learn what to do when health problems strike. I'll guide you through the maze of public and private insurers, health-care providers, and estate planning must-haves.

Chapter 12

When Crises Happen

Learning is the beginning of wealth. Learning is the beginning of health. Learning is the beginning of spirituality. Searching and learning is where the miracle process all begins.
—Jim Rohn, entrepreneur and motivational speaker

While I was traveling on business in California several years ago, I came down with acute appendicitis. I was rushed to the hospital and told that I needed an emergency appendectomy. Thankfully the procedure went along without a hitch with one exception—during my hospital stay, the staff could not find me.

Allow me to clarify. At no point during my hospitalization did I think I was lost, but later I found out what had happened. As the doctor did with all of her patients before surgery, she planned to explain the procedure to me. Unfortunately she couldn't locate me. In fact, no one in the hospital knew where I was. That is, no one except me because I was lying patiently in my hospital room. I certainly wasn't pleased to hear this news from my surgeon, mainly because the oversight added an additional day to my stay. Any frustration over that situation paled in comparison to the sticker shock that took place a few weeks later. When I was back at home, the dreaded hospital bill arrived in the mail. Removing my appendix cost a jaw-dropping $18,000. Fortunately insurance covered most of it, but I could hardly believe that my hospitalization averaged $6,000 per day. My experience illustrates what I'll address in this chapter.

There are multiple areas where things can go wrong before, during, and after a medical procedure, especially if it's an emergency. Patients may not get their medical questions answered; insurance companies, hospitals, and doctors may disagree about the best treatment for you; billing departments may make mistakes; and more.

The bottom line is that dealing with serious health problems requires two things. First, you must take complete charge of your life. Throughout this book I've emphasized the importance of assuming personal responsibility for your financial well-being. The areas addressed in this chapter, however, require a greater degree of personal responsibility because now I'm addressing both your finances *and* your health. Second, in order to ensure that the health-care system will work for rather than against you, you'll need impeccable follow-up and communication skills. In the event that you can't take on these roles yourself, you'll have to enlist others to act on your behalf.

Insurance: The Paper Trail Begins

Medical advances continue to save more lives than ever before, and doctors are performing surgeries that were unheard of even a decade ago. Today's sophisticated procedures and rising health-care costs translate to bills that can easily run into the tens of thousands and hundreds of thousands of dollars. When you're not feeling well, the last thing you want to do is spend hours on the phone with insurance companies and billing departments disputing charges. That is usually just the first step toward resolving any billing conflicts. In this section, I'll guide you through what to expect and how to effectively communicate your problems.

When you arrive at your doctor's office or the hospital, the medical staff will first ask for your insurance and, if you're sixty-five years or older, your **Medicare** card. In the ideal scenario, doctors and hospitals will bill Medicare and your insurance company directly, and both will cover the expenses according to the terms of your policy. Once payments are processed, you will be responsible for covering your deductible amount and the portion of the charges that insurance doesn't pay (called your co-pay) as well as the charges that insurance doesn't cover (called noncovered amounts). Because you're responsible for both co-pays and noncovered costs, they may seem similar, but they are completely different.

Co-pays work like this: if your plan is an 80–20 plan, after you pay your deductible the insurance company will pay 80 percent of the covered *costs,* and you pay the remaining 20 percent, hence the term co-pay. After some maximum dollar amount (for example, $5,000) is reached, the insurance company will pay 100 percent of the covered costs over that figure. On the other hand, the *noncovered* costs are exactly that—they're not covered by your insurance. They don't count toward the deductible, and they don't count toward the maximum out-of-pocket amount. Therefore, you have to pay 100 percent of these. With PPO (Preferred Provider Organization) plans it gets even more confusing. You'll come across terms such as "in network" and "out of network." "In network" means that doctors and hospitals have signed up with the PPO plan. "Out of network" means that they haven't. Take the "out of network" route and you'll pay a lot more in co-pays.

Next, you have two simple tasks. First, file any and all paperwork you receive, which can sometimes become surprisingly immense. Second, wait for Medicare and your insurance company to pay your bills. This step can take weeks. When you finally receive paperwork from your insurance company, the itemized charges and small print can be overwhelming and confusing. You'll see industry jargon such as deductibles, co-payments, allowable charges, and reasonable and customary charges.

Once insurance processes your paperwork, the doctor, hospital, and lab will send statements to you as well. If all goes smoothly, your only responsibility is to thumb through the bills and make sure that the information is accurate. Unfortunately there will often be charges that your health-care provider says it won't cover, which means that you're responsible for paying them. If you don't agree with items on the statement or you have questions, you must take the following two steps: First, contact the insurance companies and ask why they didn't cover certain parts of your doctor's bill. Second, once you receive an explanation, you need to call the billing departments of all your health-care providers to ask for a reduction in the bill based on what the insurance company told you, or to negotiate a payment plan if necessary.

The Worst Case Scenario: No Insurance

Not having health-care coverage could be financially devastating. If footing the bill for all your medical expenses far exceeds what you can afford, I suggest that you contact each medical provider, describe your current fiscal state, and then negotiate a payment plan. If you're considering declaring bankruptcy, you should share this with them. Your bankruptcy would most likely result in them receiving nothing from you. Therefore, they'd probably do their best to work out a deal so that you'd pay at least a portion of the bill.

When You Can No Longer Manage Your Finances or Medical Care on Your Own

It's possible that as a result of your medical procedures and declining health you won't be able to handle your investments and bills any longer. At this point, it may be necessary for someone else to do this for you. If you have a **revocable living trust** and a durable power of attorney, it's time for the successor you named to assume control. It is best to do this while you're still mentally competent and conscious, and it can be as simple as stating in writing your intent to resign control of your revocable trust. Note that the financial institutions in your estate may require a copy of your trust and your resignation letter.

If, on the other hand, all you have is a power of attorney, some financial institutions may require additional documents— even with this paperwork they still may refuse to recognize your successor. In some cases, the successor may have to fight courtroom battles in order to be legally recognized. Whether you have a trust, power of attorney, or both, in the event that mental incapacity has progressed *before* you're able to pass control, the successor will have to follow the steps I've described in chapters 13 and 14.

If you've handed over responsibility of your estate to your successor, and you can still communicate, it's important to continually discuss important matters with him or her. These include subjects such as bills that need to be paid, taxes that must be filed, and your overall **portfolio.** If your successor lives in another state, the Internet has made it easier than ever before for him or her to manage your accounts without having you nearby.

In regard to medical decisions, the **advance medical directive** (or **health-care power of attorney** and **living will**) makes it easy for those whom you've designated to act on your behalf. Please refer to chapter 1 for more information. If the advance medical directive, or its equivalent, isn't prepared, your family members will have to jump through significant administrative and legal hoops, which could lead to delays in making important decisions for you.

Fight for Your Rights

Have you ever been stuck in an airport because of an airline delay or cancellation? You know how frustrating it can be. The airline often won't tell you what the holdup is about unless you ask for an explanation. Despite their lack of clear communication and your lack of patience, you must assertively ask for information rather than demand it. Cross the line, and you could find yourself in serious trouble with the law. This is where an airport is like a hospital. When doctors, nurses, and staff members don't always provide the answers you're looking for, you must be able to calmly but firmly request information and updates.

No doubt when you're dealing with the health-care system, it can sometimes feel like a battle of you versus them. Understanding the point of view of your service providers may help. First off, the medical system is a large, complex, interconnected web of professionals, insurance companies, institutions, lawyers, and governments. Then there's you, the patient. Because of the complexities associated with taking care of a population as large and affluent as ours, hospitals and doctors are often treating more people than they can handle. Furthermore, insurance companies are requiring health-care providers to take care of patients expeditiously. Sometimes this forces doctors and hospitals to make decisions they don't agree with. At the same time, if they don't comply with insurers' demands, the claims may be rejected. Under these very challenging circumstances, you and your family members must follow up on the services you're provided, ask tough questions, and insist that you're receiving the best treatment.

I've witnessed first-hand mistakes that doctors and hospitals made when they treated my wife and my mother. In my wife's case, after she had her double bypass, her night shift nurse mistreated her. She had been chatting with her fellow nurses, and she was upset to have her conversation interrupted by my wife, who had requested her help. As my wife lay in bed, the nurse rolled her body over. Considering that her chest had just been sawed open on the operating table, you can imagine the pain that she experienced. Unfortunately I wasn't there to witness the event.

Shortly after, my wife told me what the nurse had done. She was feeling acute pain, but neither of us was sure whether the discomfort was a direct result of her body being abruptly moved after surgery or if it was part of the recovery process. Our uncertainty, combined with the fact that I'm typically a nonconfrontational guy, resulted in me not taking issue with what the nurse had done.

Then, shortly after my wife was released from the hospital and was recovering at home, her lungs filled with fluid—three times. Her doctors told us that this was not a typical response to bypass surgery. The draining procedure added additional misery to an already awful situation. Weeks later, when my wife and I were reflecting on the unfortunate events that took place after her surgery, we became convinced that the complications she experienced post-op were directly related to the nurse's actions. By that time, complaining to the hospital would have accomplished very little. Her procedure, full of medical mishaps, was a wake-up call to both of us.

In 2010 my mom's kidneys were failing. Having vowed never to repeat the hospital mistakes I made in the past, I enlisted the help of some friends of hers who were doctors and nurses. We all intervened by asking her primary care physician tough yet reasonable questions. In addition, a good friend who happened to be a doctor paid her a visit. As a favor to my mom, he reviewed her medications, and he immediately found potentially dangerous drug combinations. As a result, he actually changed her prescription. As you can imagine, my mom's primary care doctor wasn't pleased to have his authority threatened, but I didn't care because my mom's well-being was my top priority. It didn't stop there; we also enlisted the help of specialists.

The nephrologists (kidney specialists) proposed a course of action that would restart my mother's kidneys. It was truly a life-or-death decision because if she chose to do nothing, she wouldn't survive. To make matters worse, the procedure only had a 50 percent success rate. My mother, in her mid-eighties, decided to follow their advice, which meant that she underwent two episodes of dialysis. Fortunately the plan was a success. Although we couldn't have been happier with the result, we were appalled to learn later on that the kidney failure was completely avoidable; it occurred because of a deadly interaction between prescription drugs that she had been taking for several months.

Second Opinions and Specialists

If you're diagnosed with a potentially life-threatening disease, do yourself a favor and get a second opinion. Being proactive regarding your medical treatment could save your life. No matter how much you like your doctor, take the time to do some research and locate physicians who specialize in treating your particular illness. Keep in mind that the probability of successfully treating your disease is directly correlated to the experience and frequency with which a doctor deals with your specific illness.

With the vast amount of information available on the Internet, you can easily conduct research to locate top-rated specialists. Once you find one, ask him or her specific questions, such as: How many cases have you treated throughout your career? How many procedures or surgeries have you completed in the past year?

A colleague of mine was helping his father throughout his pancreatic cancer treatment. His dad's doctor, a primary care physician provided by his HMO, told him that the cancerous tumor was inoperable and his only option was chemo and radiation therapy. His physician added that even with chemo and radiation, he probably wouldn't live to see his next birthday—which was also an indirect way of saying that it might not even be worth the effort to undergo the treatment.

My friend immediately conducted online research. He found a physician who worked at one of approximately thirty cancer centers approved by the American Cancer Society. Fortunately, the clinic happened to be about five miles from his father's home. This doctor specialized in the Whipple procedure, which is currently the only surgery available to remove cancer in the pancreas. He performed approximately forty of these procedures each year. In addition, he was involved in ongoing research to develop new and better pancreatic cancer treatments. He met with my friend's dad, and after reviewing his case the doctor informed him that he was confident he could remove the tumor. After performing the operation, he told his patient that the cancerous tumor was relatively small and represented stage 1 cancer.

"So why did my primary care physician only give me a year to live?" he asked the specialist.

"Plain and simple," the surgeon said. "Lack of experience."

He explained that most doctors don't specialize. Therefore, they don't handle enough cases to be good at treating their patients.

Support Groups: Care Beyond Doctors and Hospitals

Part of finding the best treatment for you is to look outside the hospital and medical clinic. There are support groups and organizations that focus on particular diseases and medical problems. For example, let's say you or someone you know is battling colon cancer. If you hopped online and searched "colon cancer," you'd find multiple in-person support groups and websites and forums loaded with information ranging from dietary and nutritional recommendations to the names of top specialists in your area. The Internet is a powerful resource for information that your doctor may not have the time or inclination to share. One of my clients had cancer. After conducting Internet research, she discovered the latest nutritional research regarding her particular disease. She read that certain foods could have a major impact on her well-being. Since her release from the hospital, she has maintained a list of "foods to avoid." As a result of sticking to her dietary plan, her health has improved.

Support groups are also a place to discuss the latest treatment information. While one of my clients was attending his cancer support group, he mentioned a series of blood tests he had just taken that afternoon. The members of the group all knew intimate details of Brian's illness. As a result, one of them asked him why he hadn't requested a particular type of blood test. How was Brian supposed to know about this specific test? And why did his doctor not suggest it? The second question often relates to the course of treatment that most physicians follow.

Doctors are, in a sense, scientists, and the way scientists approach illness is to match your set of symptoms and test results with a clinical population study. The treatment will follow the path recommended under a particular study applicable to that population. While this approach has healed innumerable individuals, there's always a possibility that your condition will benefit from a different course of action. Unfortunately, deviating from the accepted path may mean that your insurance company may not cover your costs. This means that in Brian's case, even if he had requested a certain type of test, his insurance might not have paid for it. If that were to happen to me, I'd probably request the blood test as long as it was reasonable in cost, even if my insurance rejected the claim.

Diet and Exercise: Your Recovery Is in Your Hands

I've had several minor surgeries and one medical whopper—a triple bypass. The heart surgery definitely motivated me to reassess what I ate. While no one would ever confuse me for a raw-food vegan or an Atkins diet disciple, I'm a strong believer that **diet** and **exercise** are extremely important to recovery and overall wellness. Although prescription drugs can do miraculous things, most have side effects, and no medication can substitute for sound nutrition and a quality exercise program.

There are certainly circumstances where exercise is nearly impossible, but with the exception of a small group of individuals, some form is possible for most. For example, during the past several years, my church group and I have visited patients at the Walter Reed Army Medical Center in Washington, DC. We meet with soldiers who were wounded in the wars in Iraq and Afghanistan. I've seen men and women, young and not so young, with missing arms, legs, and eyes. Despite their disabilities, most of them have found a way to exercise. They recognize that it's an essential part of their recovery. I have determined that if these folks can exercise, I don't have any valid excuses not to.

If part of your healing requires changes in your diet, this too may be an enormous challenge. You may be told that you've got to increase your intake of certain foods—ones that you may not enjoy—and cut out some of your favorites. I speak from experience when I say this isn't necessarily exciting for most of us. It wasn't easy to alter my eating habits post-op, but I knew it had to happen.

I started by doing my own research and discovered that there are countless diets available. Some were so elaborate that you'd probably need Oprah's personal chef to prepare your meals, while others just didn't suit my tastes. After trial and error, and consulting with my doctor, I found a heart-healthy plan that I was able to maintain and, to my surprise, I actually learned to enjoy. My old eating habits didn't transform right away, and introducing new foods wasn't always easy. After all, our food preferences are established at an early age and reinforced over the course of our lifetimes. The experience taught me that with enough consistency, food preferences could actually change. For more recommendations related to diet and exercise, see the Toolbox.

This chapter is about common sense: address your financial and legal obligations, see your doctor, follow up with the care you receive, treat others respectfully, take your prescription medications, exercise, and eat healthy. It's simple advice that is by no means easy, but all of it is absolutely essential in order to effectively deal with health-care crises.

In the next chapter, we'll continue on the theme of health with a focus on the mind. How do you plan ahead to handle mental incapacity?

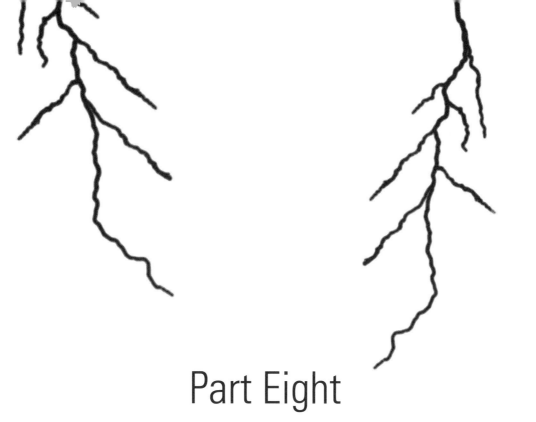

Part Eight

What If I Lost My Mind?

Chapter 13

For the Parents—Your Second Choice

The journey into dementia has its disappointments to be endured as well as its triumphs to be cherished. In all of the ambiguities and confusion there may also be signs of hope, for this is a journey with intersecting signposts; reminders of the past and pointers to the future. There are always fresh opportunities for a new walk on a new day.
—Rosalie Hudson, associate professor,
University of Melbourne and Aged Care Consultant

Independence. It's one of the hallmarks of being an American. The simple and inevitable truth, though, is that when mental incapacity strikes, you'll be completely at the mercy of other people. In fact, as fiercely self-sufficient as most of us aspire to be, you probably know a family member or a close friend who is or will become disabled. So the question I ask you is this: "If living at home would be impossible due to your deteriorating mental condition, what would your *second choice* be?" If you don't plan ahead, someone else will most likely make that decision for you, and you probably won't be as happy with the outcome as you would have been had you called the shots.

Consider the following facts: one out of ten men and one out of five women will develop dementia or Alzheimer's disease. For anyone who reaches eight-five years of age, the likelihood jumps to 50 percent. In my mother-in-law's case, her dementia worsened to the point where she could no longer live on her own. After a short stint in an assisted living facility, she eventually came to live with my wife and me. Our home is where she died just before Christmas in 2008.

Illness due to mental incapacity is not easy on anyone. However, there are steps you can take ahead of time to lessen the difficulties on yourself and those around you. In this chapter, you'll learn how to address the *residential*, *legal*, and *financial* aspects of your life—*before* debilitating illnesses strike.

The Cast of Characters: Parents and Children

Our country is aging. This may seem like nothing new, but it actually is. Advances in medicine are extending our lives unlike any other time in human history. This means that we're living longer, often with health conditions that would have spelled immediate death for our ancestors. As life spans have increased, so have the odds that we'll eventually lose the ability to function on our own, which means that at some point we'll need additional help, either in our homes or in some type of care facility.

No doubt adjusting to change when it comes to our deteriorating mental states will be enormously stressful for everyone involved. Through my own experience dealing with elderly parents and my professional work helping my clients, I've seen the rewards of planning ahead and the consequences of putting things off until it's too late.

In order to decrease confusion as I illustrate my points, I've simplified the cast of characters in the long-term care drama. Throughout this chapter, they'll be called the following:

- **Parents:** These are the people who are in need of long-term care; they are usually senior citizens.
- **Children:** These are the individuals who will be supporting Parents. They are often adult children, extended family members, friends, or a combination of all three.

Parents are responsible for the initial planning. The more time and resources they commit to this, the happier their situation will be for everyone later on. The less planning they do, the more their own happiness decreases, and the bigger the problems will be for Children.

The Three Categories of Planning

Being old, sick, and broke is one of the most painful consequences of not planning ahead. When you can no longer take care of yourself, meeting your needs will require money—and often lots of it. If you're out of money, you may have no choice but to apply for **Medicaid**, which is our government-run poverty health program for people with low incomes, few resources, or both. In this section, I'll explain the three categories you must consider when planning ahead: *residential*, *legal*, and *financial*.

Residential

Shelter is a basic human necessity. Although the concept is simple, in our modern, complex society, there are multiple options when it comes to Parents who are mentally incapacitated. To start, there are two broad categories: stay at home or not. As obvious as this point may seem, the stay-at-home and residential options are vast and complex.

Four Stay-at-Home Choices

For the most part, Parents prefer to live in their own homes independently and without intervention from others. This is referred to as "aging in place" and "staying at home." Parents comprise the fastest-growing group in North America, and they are also at the highest risk of needing care. The following are a Parent's four stay-at-home options (remember that I'm using "Parents" to refer to a specific group):

- **Family and friends' assistance:** This is the easiest to understand. If you've ever accompanied a Parent to a doctor's appointment, then you've taken part in this to some extent already. Or an adult child may move into a Parent's home and provide care for the Parent. Alternatively, as with my mother-in-law, the Parent might move into a Child's home.

- **Privately hired caregivers:** Perhaps someone you trust is looking for extra work. This could be a person who lives in the neighborhood, attends your church or synagogue, or you know through some other avenue. If you have a great deal of confidence in the person, and he or she is reliable and caring, then hiring this person can be a cost-effective decision. You must consider the tax and insurance consequences of choosing this option, however. For example, the Parent will have to apply for an *Employer Identification Number* (EIN) from the IRS and provide a W-2 to the caregiver by January 31 of each year for the amount paid to the person. In addition, the Parent will have to file

> An EIN is either your Social Security number or another taxpayer identification number issued by the IRS.

Schedule H on his or her 1040 tax return, and pay Social Security and **Medicare** tax on the amount paid to the caregiver.

- **Professional caregivers:** Hiring dependable and expert caregivers is the best solution for many families. These individuals are trained, insured, bonded, and licensed. Furthermore, the businesses that the caregivers work for will handle taxes, insurance, days off, and more. There is no EIN or Schedule H to deal with.

- **Adult daycare.** These are senior care centers that are designed to provide companionship and a social outlet for seniors. The daycare facilities do this through activities that are planned throughout the day. They *do not* offer one-on-one care. Parents who participate in adult daycare live in either their own homes or their Children's homes and spend their daytime hours at the center.

Five Residential Options for Parents Who Can No Longer Stay at Home

The following options exist for those who cannot maintain their own home and are not able to move in with a family member:

- **Independent senior living facilities:** These are communities for seniors looking for social activities, maintenance-free housing, and prepared meals. They *do not* provide care, but they often arrange for professional caregivers to assist those who need it. Think of independent senior living like an apartment community for seniors. Like any apartment, residents are responsible for paying monthly rent. Long-term care insurance does not cover these expenses.

- **Assisted living:** This is a step beyond independent senior living. In addition to activities and meals, assisted living facilities also offer bathing and dressing assistance and medication management. Because of the extensive care they provide, assisted living typically costs from two to four times more than independent senior living. LTCI may cover some of these expenses if, for instance, a Parent cannot perform two or more Activities of Daily Living (I explained ADLs in chapter 11).

- **Residential care homes:** These are a hybrid of professional caregivers and assisted living communities. These are small private homes that have from three to eight residents who live together and share meals. Caregivers are employed to assist with bathing, dressing, and medication management. This option is usually more expensive than assisted living. LTCI would probably cover many of the residential care home costs because a Parent could not perform two or more ADLs.

- **Continuing Care Retirement Communities (CCRC), also called Life Care Communities:** These offer a tiered approach to care that starts off at the independent living level and adjusts as the Parent's health declines. This means that there is a continuum of services that includes housing and nursing care. When Parents move to a CCRC, they can continue to live there regardless of what happens to their health. The costs are contractually predetermined. LTCI would cover expenses when a Parent couldn't perform two or more ADLs.

- **Nursing homes:** These are designed for those who require significant skilled care due to an illness, chronic condition, or hospital discharge. Nursing homes often appear less residential and more hospital-like because they provide the highest level of care of all the residential options. Medicare pays for nursing home care for a set period of time, usually only one hundred days if it is ordered and supervised by a physician. Beyond one hundred days, however, the financial burden falls on the Parents and Children. LTCI would cover expenses because a Parent could not perform two or more ADLs. Some LTCI policies, however, would pay simply on the basis of a Parent being in a nursing home (this will be stipulated in the insurance policy). Check your policy for details. If there is still not enough money to cover costs, a Parent's only alternative may be to seek Medicaid if the Child cannot afford to pay. More on this in the "Financial" section of this chapter.

In many instances, Parents will experience a combination of these five residential options. In addition, there is a high likelihood that there will be a progression from one type to another. The word "progression" may be misleading, though, because one unfortunate fact you must understand is that *your loved ones will not get better.* It's an important but difficult mental and emotional hurdle to get over.

Parents, Make Your Wishes Known

A Parent's desire to die in his or her own home can lead to enormous problems depending on their particular situation. For example, a Parent's neighborhood may be in decline, his or her house may not be equipped to accommodate a Parent's physical limitations, the Parent may not be able to attend to basic needs such as food, or Children may live far away.

Therefore Parents should express a preferred second option. If not, they'll force their Children to make life-altering decisions that may go against their wishes. This may result in arguments and emotional trauma.

For example, I've worked with Children whose Parents were in steady mental decline. Despite, or sometimes because of, their compromised mental condition, the Parents absolutely refused to leave their homes. The Children found themselves in the very stressful position of having to force Parents to move out of their own homes and into one of the residential options I described above.

On the bright side, I've worked with Parents who planned ahead, which made life easier for everyone involved. One client decided that she wanted to move into a Continuing Care Retirement Community while she was still relatively healthy. Maria already had friends living in the complex, and they had given it a hearty endorsement. Maria and I analyzed the various cost options, and once she decided that she wanted to move in, we determined the steps that she needed to take. First, in order to meet the CCRC's significant down payment, she had to sell her present home, but her monthly payment to the CCRC was less than her previous housing (including homeowner's insurance and property taxes) and food expenses. Once she moved in, Maria and her children had peace of mind knowing that she would be well taken care of throughout her retirement.

Legal

In chapter 1, I explained that every adult should have a trust, will, power of attorney, **advance medical directive**, and, in many cases, **life insurance**. Please review chapter 1 because the five fundamentals of an estate plan are key to providing for you in the event that you become mentally incapacitated. If you have these taken care of, then you can be confident that the right people—those you know, love, and trust—will be making the best possible decisions on your behalf. If, on the other hand, these estate planning essentials aren't prepared, you'll be at the mercy of judges, courts, and lawyers, and you will create unnecessary delays and expenses for your children.

Allow me to expand on one of the five fundamentals as it applies to mental incapacity. As the name indicates, the advance medical directive takes care of medical and health decisions. On the other hand, the **revocable living trust** and durable power of attorney deal with financial issues and decisions. These terms often get confused because some states utilize a health-care power of attorney in addition to the durable power of attorney. An easy way to clear up the confusion is to remember that if it has "health care" in its name, then that's all that it has power over.

Financial

Neglecting to thoroughly address finances could result in Parents running out of cash, which may force them to turn to others for support. If the Children's resources aren't sufficient, it may become necessary for Parents to become impoverished in order to qualify for Medicaid, which is a government-funded welfare program. (Remember, Medicaid is *not* Medicare.) Unfortunately this could result in a legal mess for Parents. In the last several decades, laws have been passed that have made dubious strategies to qualify for Medicaid benefits not only a bad idea but criminal as well.

If Parents give away their assets to their Children in hopes that the state won't get its hands on them, Parents should know that every state has a "look-back" period that will bring those assets back in the Medicaid eligibility calculation. On the other hand, if Parents give away all their money and assets five years before they apply for Medicaid, that's a very long time to be completely financially dependent on the good graces of other family members. There are much better ways to cover the financial costs of mental incapacity. The following are three: long-term care insurance, various sources of income, and selling assets.

Long-Term Care Insurance (LTCI)

Please refer to chapter 11, where I illustrate the benefits and costs of LTCI.

Various Sources of Income

If Parents are in such a state that they can't take care of themselves anymore, they won't be spending money on many of the things they bought throughout their adult lives. In fact, Parents can probably scan nearly every category in their budget right now and see that many of their expenses will be irrelevant once they can't take care of themselves. For example, they won't have car expenses, won't be going out to dinner, and won't be taking vacations. If Parents continue to stay at home, then clearly their home maintenance expenses will continue. If they move in with Children or choose one of the non-stay-at-home residential options, then the costs associated with maintaining their homes will disappear. This means that if Parents have adequate health insurance, their living expenses may actually go down. While this will not always be the case, Parents shouldn't automatically assume that the costs of long-term care will be *in addition* to the items in their current budget.

Now that I've explained the possibility of decreases in living expenses, I'll list various sources of income that will pay for long-term care costs:

- Social Security benefits
- Pension income
- Veteran's benefits
- IRA or retirement plan required minimum distributions (withdrawals)
- Investment income (interest, dividends, **capital gains**, and more)
- Rental income (either from rental properties Parents already own or by renting out a room in their home)

In order to determine whether a Parent has enough income to cover the cost of his or her care, simply add up the monthly income from Social Security, pensions, required withdrawals from retirement plans, and veteran's benefits. Next, calculate a sustainable withdrawal rate from nonretirement investment assets. If the total isn't enough, then Parents must sell some of their assets, which leads us to the next section.

Sell Assets

Everything a Parent owns now needs to be evaluated. So where do Parents start? I suggest that they begin by reviewing their bank and investment accounts. Next, if they own real estate, they should consider planning for the eventual sale of property. By real estate, I'm referring to both the home where they live and any investment property they possess. As far as their own homes are concerned, if Parents won't be living there anymore, there's no reason to keep them—unless they can rent them out, find someone to manage the property, and generate rental income that far exceeds maintenance and mortgage expenses.

Your Long-Term Care Checklist

To adequately plan ahead, Parents need to do the following:

- Legally name the person(s) who will make medical decisions on their behalf.
- Legally specify the person(s) who will handle their finances in the event that Parents become incompetent—both as successor trustees of their trusts and as successor power of attorney (attorney-in-fact).
- Develop and analyze a cash flow projection of their income and expenses (including taxes). This would be a what-if scenario that, for example, assumes Parents would need nursing home care for ten years. As a result, Parents will have a clear picture of what the future will look like financially. It will enable them to make good decisions because they can see whether or not they'll run out of money. If the first analysis does not look good, Parents can consider additional what-if scenarios until they come up with a financial plan that has a high probability of not running out of money.
- If their income and assets aren't sufficient, Parents need to research long-term care insurance options if it's not too late—that is, if their health has not deteriorated to the point they are uninsurable (which means the insurance company declines their application and will not issue them a policy—at any price).

Overwhelmed? Consider Consulting an Expert

Long-term nursing care, mental disability, and selling off your most prized possessions—these aren't the topics of feel-good conversations. This is why most people put off planning until it's too late. If you've hit a mental roadblock and you find yourself unable to move forward, an expert may be able to provide much-needed support. A competent CFP® Professional will help you project your future expenses and determine your available income and assets. With this information, you'll know whether you'll have enough cash to meet your needs in the event of mental incapacity. If you determine that you won't have enough income, your CFP® Professional will recommend ways to meet the costs of long-term care.

In the next chapter, Children will be in charge. We'll explore how they'll meet the needs of Parents who are mentally incapacitated.

Chapter 14

For the Children—Meeting the Needs

Ronnie's long journey has finally taken him to a distant place where I can no longer reach him.
—Nancy Reagan, wife of former president Ronald Reagan, 1911–2004, who was stricken with Alzheimer's in 1994
As quoted in the Baltimore Sun, June 7, 2004

A uthor's Warning: this will be the most melancholy chapter of all. Why? Because caring for and making decisions on behalf of aging and incompetent Parents is *never fun*. To make matters worse, their health will only further deteriorate. In addition, the very nature of their disability means that Parents won't be able to take on most of the responsibilities that you'll learn about and the burden will fall squarely on Children and other caregivers.[21] The bright side is that knowledge is power. In this chapter, I'll shed light on the aspects of old age that are often shrouded in silence, secrecy, and even shame.

---

21. You'll notice that I've made Parents and Children proper nouns. If you're wondering why, please refer to chapter 13, where I provide a definition of who these people are.

The Difference Between Death and Disability

During a routine client meeting, a client shared that her mother's Alzheimer's had gotten much worse since we had last met. It had already been five years since she was first diagnosed with the disease, and now my client and her brother were running out of cash to take care of their mom.

"I envy my friends whose parents died suddenly," she told me. She knew that her friends had suffered immensely after their parents had passed, but unlike her, their grieving process had a beginning and an end.

"For my brother and me, it's like a wound that won't heal. A scab appears, then it gets ripped off right away," she said.

Her mom's mental decline had also strained her relationship with her brother. Because their mother had run out of savings, the two children were responsible for covering her expenses. My client was resentful toward her mom for not planning better, and she was angry with her brother because she believed that he wasn't providing enough financial support. Meanwhile, he maintained that he didn't have the money to help out more.

A Dip in Financial IQ Is a Dementia Red Flag

The gradual decline that typically signals clinical dementia makes it an illness that's difficult to assess. In addition, Children often psychologically choose to ignore the symptoms rather than acknowledge a Parent's mental deterioration. Furthermore, the denial causes Children and Parents to delay thinking of a future that seems to only spell doom and gloom.

So what are some of the dementia warning signs? Look out for a Parent who is no longer able to manage finances. A 2010

New York Times article, "Money Woes Can Be Early Clue to Alzheimer's" reported that "confusion over money and finances is perhaps the most important and most predictable early functional change as people descend into dementia."[22] In its early stages, dementia may cause Parents to make uncharacteristically terrible financial decisions. For instance, they can fall prey to financial scams and solicitors seeking charitable contributions or buy things they see on TV shopping channels. By the time Children intervene, a Parent's savings may have taken a hit or, in extreme cases, be wiped out completely as a result of mismanagement.

Even if a Parent works with a financial advisor, CPA, estate planning attorney, or all three, and they observe possible signs of mental decline, the service providers may not inform the Children. In fact, many professionals feel uncomfortable bringing up their concerns to their clients directly, let alone sharing the news with nonclient family members. One reason for their silence is a legal or regulatory issue having to do with client confidentiality agreements.

At The Monitor Group, we have developed a written policy regarding how we will deal with clients who have dementia and with whom we will share information if we have sufficient evidence our client is in mental decline.

Because of such confidentiality issues, Children must be observant and ready to act on behalf of Parents. The first step Children can take to snap out of denial and into action is to enlist the support of a Parent's primary care physician. One approach is for a Child to accompany the Parent to a routine doctor's appointment. This will give the Child an opportunity to bring up their concerns to the physician. The doctor may refer the patient to a geriatric specialist, who will diagnose a Parent's

22. Gina Kolata, "Money Woes Can Be Early Clue to Alzheimer's," New York Times, October 30, 2010.

current state and, if it is dementia, will most likely prescribe medication. It's very important that Children make sure that Parents are taking their meds—they actually can help quite a bit. Often there will be several pills to swallow every day, which can be difficult to keep track of. An easy solution is to buy a plastic pillbox that has compartments for every day of the week. Other people prefer written instructions.

The Loss of Freedom: Driving and Living Arrangements

At some point, the role of caretaker (Parent) and dependent (Child) are uncomfortably reversed. The Child is forced, by the risk of potentially serious harm to a Parent and others, to make choices that go against their Parent's wishes and limit the Parent's freedom, which affects the Parent's perceived quality of life. The Children recognize the decisions they must make and know what they must do but often choose to delay the decision-making so the Parent will not be angry with them; in addition, Children are very concerned that their actions will actually cause a more rapid decline.

Eventually Children must confiscate a Parent's car keys. This can be an emotionally devastating decision, but the consequences of maintaining the status quo could be life-threatening. My wife and her siblings struggled with how to address this matter with their mom. My wife lived hundreds of miles away from her mother, while her sister and brother lived in the same town as Mom. Her sister would periodically call with reports of their mother "slipping" or people calling to say they saw her run a red light.

From a distance, it was clear to my wife that their mother should no longer be driving and she told her sister she should take the keys away from mom. Her sister resisted because the impact of this action would fall on her. She would be the one with whom the mother would be angry; she would have the guilt of limiting her mother's freedom and possibly accelerate mom's descent into the black hole of dementia. Their brother left the decision-making up to the sisters, deferring to the mother–daughter relationship. The siblings continued the phone calls discussing options, which included getting a doctor to officially diagnose dementia (proven to be more challenging than it appears) and using the DMV (department of motor vehicles) regulations to take her license away, thereby deflecting responsibility for that decision away from the Children.

In the midst of all this, their mother turned into the mall parking lot from a four-lane road and hit a young man on his motorcycle. They knew that something like this might happen, but they had avoided the conversation with Mom because they didn't want to hurt her feelings. Thankfully, he survived, but he sustained injuries that would affect him for the rest of his life. In hindsight, the siblings understood that their delay in firm decision-making was not exclusively a problem for them with implications for their mother, but also carried needless and potentially grave consequences for others.

Tragically the man and his family would feel the impact of this accident for the rest of their lives. His insurance company sued my wife's mother. Fortunately, her insurance was sufficient to cover the lawsuit and insurance claim. If the insurance had not been adequate for the judgment against her, the siblings would have been forced to sell their mother's assets to pay the court's charging order. If that were the case, it would have had further consequences by financially reducing the choices for quality of life in the parent's remaining years.

There are frequent stories in the news of older persons who harm or kill others because they drive when they should not. You may remember the senior who pressed the accelerator rather than the brake and killed many in a street market in California some years ago.

The conversation won't be easy, but not having it for fear of hurting a Parent's feelings is no excuse. For some, the result of the conversation is the Parent understanding that the Children are speaking the truth in love and hand over the car keys. For others, it may be like my wife's family when her sister took the car keys away. Their mother, hanging onto her freedom with all her might, cleverly anticipated this might happen and had six spare keys made and then hid them in the house. She used one of those spare keys on that fateful day. The car was towed to a repair facility, and when it was fixed the sisters gave the car to their brother so that it could not be accessed by their mother again.

A more firm decision when the siblings were first made aware that the Parent's thinking was impaired would have included removing the car at the outset, but every step is equally as painful for the Children and is often done in smaller increments that are more comfortable for them. In weighing risk to the Parent or others, it is important to make decisions in the interest of greatest safety for all concerned and not on emotion rooted in the desire to have everything remain as it always appeared to the Child within: that the parent was strong, wise, and immortal. The right decisions, firmly made, are a reflection of great love and preserve the ability to make better quality-of-life decisions for their parent.

Housing is no less difficult and has many and varied options, creating challenges not seen with the driving dilemma. Who among us would not first desire to remain in our homes, which are filled with memories and have been the place of our great joys and sorrows? Safety once again must become our pivot point and financials the limiting factors for decision making. Further complicating the process is the knowledge that every decision short of a nursing home is temporary and fluid in timing. It is like playing chess and anticipating your next move based upon the move made by your parent's mental and physical health, length of life, and how long their money lasts. So as far as housing is concerned, the Parent will most likely want to remain in his or her home—despite the risks of maintaining the current living arrangement.

If a Parent's spouse is still alive, and he or she is healthy, then the spouse may be able to take on the duties of caring for the ailing Parent. But a Parent's condition will get worse, which means that a spouse, Children, or both will eventually have to hire outside help. They may enlist an in-home caregiver who will work several hours a day or, if necessary, twenty-four hours a day, which becomes expensive very quickly. It is helpful to do a financial analysis at this point (see chapter 2) to assess various living and care arrangements, considering the income, savings and investments, taxes, and total costs of the proposed arrangement.

Hire Help

When caring for Parents becomes overwhelming, Children can enlist the help of a social worker or **geriatric care manager**. These professionals begin by drafting a formal assessment that outlines the Parent's health, living situation, finances, and other factors. They will use the assessment as a guide to create a custom care plan. Social workers and geriatric care managers can also arrange care services, provide referrals, locate community resources, and answer essential questions. They usually charge from $250 to $750 for an initial assessment and from $50 to $200 per hour for ongoing consulting. Unfortunately **Medicare**, **Medicaid**, and insurance rarely cover the cost of social workers and geriatric care managers. To find one, check with your local government under "Department for the Aging" or a similar name. There may also be **Area Agencies on Aging** (AAAs) that can help you find the resources you need.

Long-Term Care Insurance (LTCI) and Power of Attorney

Please refer to chapter 11, where I address how to begin the LTCI claims process. In chapter 12, I also explain how the successor trustee goes about taking charge of a Parent's finances. To effectively manage both power of attorney and LTCI, Children must get organized. There will be claim forms to submit, and it may be necessary to save receipts and submit them to LTCI providers for reimbursement. Not all expenses are eligible, so it's important to know which receipts to keep. If Children already have an effective money management system in place, they should implement it rather than try to figure out their Parent's method. A simple suggestion is to buy a folder that has dividers inside. Using this will help Children keep track of statements such as savings, checking, credit card, and investment accounts; medical bills from hospitals, doctors, clinics, and Medicare; and supplementary insurance.

Simplify the Estate

By the time Parents are showing signs of mental deterioration, they may have assembled a sophisticated **portfolio** comprising significant assets. It may include multiple insurance policies, investment accounts that are decades old, and several savings accounts. Once Children take charge, figuring out their Parent's estate could be a daunting task. Now it's time to simplify the portfolio in order for Parents to maintain a certain degree of independence, protect their financial security, and make it easier for Children to effectively manage their money.

> An after-tax account is an investment account that is not a retirement account. Taxes have already been paid on the money invested in an after-tax account.

The following are steps to simplify the estate:

1. If there are savings, checking, and money market accounts and CDs open at different banks, merge the multiple accounts and keep them at one financial institution.

2. Consolidate investment accounts under one custodian, such as Schwab, TD Ameritrade, Fidelity, etc. If Parents are working with a CFP® Professional, and Children are confident of the advisor's credibility and competence, they should use the advisor's custodian.

3. Only have one IRA per Parent and one *after-tax account* registered to the Parent's trust (or both Parents' trusts jointly as tenants in common).

4. Pay off loans that have high interest rates or low balances.

5. Pare down credit cards to one—two or three at most.

6. Set up online financial institution accounts.

7. When the temptation arises to maintain (not deal with) a complicated estate or make it even more complex, repeat the mantra, "Minimize, minimize, minimize!"

Create a Budget

The next step is for Children to develop a budget and figure out how to make payments. A preliminary step is to determine which monthly expenses are automatically deducted from checking and credit card accounts. Thankfully online account management and bill pay have made this much easier—although it's still time-consuming. In order to have direct access to accounts, Children need to show financial institutions the power of attorney and the trust document. It's best to have Parents resign as trustees while they are still competent and before any incompetence has set in. Otherwise, Children may have to submit proof based on the criteria outlined in the trust. Sometimes Children may have to go as far as to have three independent doctors verify incompetence. In addition, attorneys sometimes handle the resignation. Usually this means that a lawyer will quiz a parent to determine his or her client's competence.

> Insurance reimbursements occur when the health insurance company pays the doctor or hospital bill or sends you a check after you paid the bill.

A durable power of attorney does not require a resignation or any form of evidence. However, many financial institutions won't accept it; consider this the rule rather than the exception. I've had clients who dealt with banks and **mutual fund** companies that required the power of attorney to be certified to be current *each time* they attempted to use it. As you can imagine, this can be immensely inconvenient. So when anyone claims that a power of attorney solves everything, take this more as fantasy than fact.

When it comes to taxes, Children should assemble all of a Parent's relevant tax data and file a Parent's income tax return on behalf of him or her. This means that the person with the power of attorney will sign the tax return. LTCI benefits are tax-free income, and medical expenses are deductible above a certain threshold, but this excludes *insurance reimbursements.* In addition, Activities of Daily Living (ADLs), which I described in chapter 11, are referenced in the Internal Revenue Code. Hiring someone to assist with ADLs is a deductible expense if the person has been certified as "chronically ill" by a licensed health care practitioner and the personal care services are provided pursuant to a written plan prescribed by the practitioner.

A CPA can certainly help with tax preparation, but it's ultimately the Children's responsibility to collect documents and keep track of a Parent's income and expenses.

A Financial Advisor's Continuity of Service

If a Parent had enough foresight to consult with a CFP® Professional, then Children should schedule a meeting with him or her to determine a **cash flow plan**. This will be based on Parent's investments, other assets, and the budget that he or she already had in place.

Do you recall TIME from chapter 5? *T* stands for Time, *I* represents Interest, *M* stands for Millions, and *E* refers to Emotions. This means that if a Parent has substantial assets but doesn't have a CFP® Professional, then Children should hire one. After all, maintaining a Parent's physical well-being is enough responsibility, let alone managing a complex investment portfolio that will have to generate enough cash every month to cover bills. In the end, a competent professional will decrease a Child's stress and make life easier for everyone.

Possible Pitfalls between Family Members

One of my clients was accused of taking antique furniture from his mother's home. His sister was furious and equated his action with stealing. My client admitted to removing the furniture, but he insisted that his mother had given it to him. That was one of the many issues that arose throughout their mother's illness. Sadly, years have passed since their mother died, and the siblings still refuse to speak to one another. Conflicts like these can ruin family relationships forever.

What I often see is that the Child who assumes most of the money management duties is accused by his or her siblings of mismanaging a Parent's estate. Often these bad-tempered brothers and sisters aren't lifting a finger to help out. It's a sad but true scenario. Siblings will often bicker over investment decisions that a Child made or moneymaking opportunities that the Child missed.

The following are two scenarios that have a high likelihood of creating conflict:

- A Child seeks fiscal security, so she sells all stocks and mutual funds and transfers the proceeds to regular bank savings accounts. Shortly after, the stock market quickly ascends. Or the opposite occurs . . .

- A Child sees opportunity to increase the value of a Parent's portfolio and takes funds from regular savings accounts and invests the money in stocks and mutual funds. As soon as the funds are transferred, the stock market plummets. This is another good reason to hire a competent, caring CFP® Professional who will help you make critical investment decisions. As I pointed out in chapter 5, individual investors tend to do the wrong thing at the wrong time.

The Truth Sometimes Hurts, but It Will Also Set You Free

As a CFP® Professional who is committed to the well-being of my clients, I understand the challenges that Parents and Children face when it comes to mental decline. I've witnessed brothers and sisters work together to provide their sick parent the highest quality of life possible. I've also seen siblings torn apart by greed and anger, despite a Parent's best efforts to prepare an estate before mental incapacity struck. It's these experiences, both good and bad, that have allowed me to guide you through the process of effectively dealing with the realities of dementia.

Conclusion

There's an old joke that goes like this: "How do you make God laugh? Make a plan!"

This book has been all about planning ahead and then dealing with reality. I'm a planner. It's what I do. Yet I fully realize no one can plan away all of life's potential problems. Yes, good planning can in some cases help us avoid problems entirely; indeed, big mistakes can be circumvented. In most cases, good planning helps us make good decisions ahead of time, and then makes whatever trouble floods our lives a little easier to navigate.

It is very important to plan ahead. It is prudent and wise. Make no mistake—we cannot see the future and thus create plans that will make our lives rosy and trouble-free forever.

Dealing with reality actually has two parts. I have only dealt with the first part in this book; that is, the practical solutions to real-life tragedies and difficulties. The other facet of dealing with reality is much more complex and beyond the scope of this book. I'm talking about the intellectual, emotional, and spiritual aspects of dealing with the reality of evil in this world.

Each of us has our own opinions about these issues. Rather than delve into what I believe, in this conclusion I will simply tell you about some resources that have been helpful to me.

None of this will be easy, light reading, but the issues of pain, suffering, and loss are not light subjects. A very popular book written in the early 1980s was *When Bad Things Happen to Good People* by Harold Kushner. While I am not in complete agreement with Rabbi Kushner on some of his conclusions, I do know this book has been quite helpful to many people.

I recommend two other books for your consideration. The first is *The Problem of Pain* by C. S. Lewis, an Oxford scholar and Cambridge professor, and an atheist until his conversion to Christianity; he also wrote the Narnia series. In this book is Lewis's well-known quote: "God whispers to us in our pleasures, speaks in our conscience, but shouts in our pains; it is His megaphone to rouse a deaf world." The second book, *Affliction* by Edith Schaeffer, is an evangelical look at the question of dealing with tragedy and suffering.

There are a couple of resources by master theologian, philosopher, and teacher R.C. Sproul, of Ligonier Ministries in Orlando, Florida, that I have particularly enjoyed. First, a teaching series available on CD or MP3 download titled *The Providence of God* is very good. Second, for a comprehensive historical summary of philosophical thought from before Socrates to recent philosophers of modernism, I highly recommend Sproul's book *The Consequences of Ideas* or the teaching series on CD/MP3 download based on this book.

You may think all this philosophical or religious stuff is nonsense, and life strikes are really just due to fate or chance. Well, consider this: the term "chance" is simply a mathematical term that describes probabilities. For example, what is the chance that a flipped coin will land on "heads"? The probability (chance) is 50 percent. But "chance" cannot cause anything. Chance is not a self-existent being with causal power; rather, it is a descriptive term. Chance has no power or causal force. Chance is not a thing—chance is no thing—chance is nothing![23]

So personally, I think there's more to it than that.

My desire is that you will adequately plan for the various life strikes that could harm you physically, emotionally, financially, and spiritually. I want you to be able to deal with them in a practical sense, but I believe it would be beneficial if you are also able to deal with these issues in a grounded intellectual and spiritual sense. Emerging from life strikes as a confident, joyful person with an optimistic outlook and an assurance of hope will mean your life will be full and abundant. The alternative is to live with anger, bitterness, blaming others (or God), cynicism, or denial. All of those end badly.

You may have heard the beatitude, "Blessed are those who mourn, for they shall be comforted."[24] This comfort can come in this life, and I believe in the life to come. It can come in this life if you have the proper mindset, or attitude, with respect to the tragedies you face. Mourning has mysterious powers—it builds character, causes you to gain perspective, and opens you up to new ways of thinking and feeling. You are better able to understand, empathize with, and counsel others who are going through the same difficult things you have experienced.

This book has addressed planning for the future and dealing with reality. No, you cannot plan away every tragedy. On the contrary, the probabilities are high that you will go through one or more of the "life strikes" mentioned in this book. You cannot avoid them, but you can minimize the impact and the expense on you or your loved ones by doing

---

23. R.C. Sproul, The Providence of God, 1990.
24. Matthew 5:4

some good planning. If you deal with the reality of these "life strikes" properly, you can avoid even more emotional and psychological pain and suffering.

I pray you will be blessed and happy.

Appendix: Financial Toolbox

Advance Medical Directive

In many states, an advance medical directive combines two documents: the living will and the health-care power of attorney. Basically, a living will says, "Pull the plug under the following circumstances . . ." This is important to people who adhere to particular cultural and religious beliefs. For instance, I've had Roman Catholic clients who outlined specific wishes regarding the terms under which they would end life. The health-care power of attorney gives legal authority for someone to make all kinds of medical decisions on your behalf.

The Commonwealth of Virginia authorized advance medical directives in 1992 as a result of federal legislation that required health providers to inform their patients of their rights regarding medical decisions in case of incapacity. Some states, however, do not use advance medical directives. In those cases, you must get both a living will and health-care power of attorney. Hospitals and other medical institutions will, over time, become used to seeing the advance medical directive. It's more likely to be accepted over health-care powers that are linked with financial matters.

A benefit of an advance medical directive or health-care power of attorney is that you can appoint someone to be an attorney-in-fact for medical decisions and another person to be the attorney-in-fact of the general durable power of attorney. Why is this important? Many people have a family member or advisor who would be the best person to help them with financial and business affairs, while a different person may be best suited to deal with health decisions.

On a final note, it's important that your documents conform with the Health Insurance Portability and Accountability Act of 1996 (also known as HIPAA). There are privacy restrictions that doctors and hospitals take very seriously, and you want to make sure they accept your legal documents.

Area Agencies on Aging (AAA)

Area Agencies on Aging were established under the Older Americans Act (OAA) in 1973 to respond to the needs of Americans throughout the country who were sixty years of age and older. According to their website, "by providing a range of options that allow older adults to choose the home- and community-based services and living arrangements that suit them best, AAAs make it possible for older adults to remain in their homes and communities as long as possible." For more information and many helpful resources, visit the AAA's website at www.n4a.org.

Asset Allocation (Diversification)

The following explanations of asset allocation are excerpts from the "Beginners' Guide to Asset Allocation, Diversification, and Rebalancing," a free publication presented online by the US

Securities and Exchange Commission (SEC), which regulates financial institutions:

Asset Allocation 101: Asset allocation involves dividing an investment portfolio among different asset categories, such as stocks, bonds, and cash. The process of determining which mix of assets to hold in your portfolio is a very personal one. The asset allocation that works best for you at any given point in your life will depend largely on your time horizon and your ability to tolerate risk.

The Magic of Diversification: The practice of spreading money among different investments to reduce risk is known as diversification. By picking the right group of investments, you may be able to limit your losses and reduce the fluctuations of investment returns without sacrificing too much potential gain.

Why Asset Allocation Is So Important: By including asset categories with investment returns that move up and down under different market conditions within a portfolio, an investor can protect against significant losses. Historically, the returns of the three major asset categories have not moved up and down at the same time. Market conditions that cause one asset category to do well often cause another asset category to have average or poor returns. By investing in more than one asset category, you'll reduce the risk that you'll lose money and your portfolio's overall investment returns will have a smoother ride.

For the remainder of this guide, including information on short-term versus long-term financial goals, visit: www.sec.gov/investor/pubs/assetallocation.htm.

See also **investment choices**, **modern portfolio theory**, **mutual fund**, **portfolio**, **rebalancing**, **risk versus reward**, and **stock selection**.

Beneficiary

A beneficiary is a person who benefits from the assets of another person (a "benefactor"). If you were the named beneficiary of another person's life insurance policy or a retirement plan, you would receive that money when the person died. Also, trusts have named beneficiaries, who will receive income, principal, or both from the trust under the specific conditions written in the trust document.

The primary beneficiary or beneficiaries receive the money unless they are deceased or do not qualify for some other reason. In those instances, the money will go to the "contingent" (successor) beneficiaries named in the contract (life insurance policy, retirement plan, or trust).

Generally, if you are receiving assets (cash or other property) as a beneficiary, the money is passing by contract. Thus it is not subject to probate.

It's important to regularly review all of your beneficiary designations, such as insurance policies, IRAs, retirement plans at work, transfer-on-death or payable-on-death investment accounts, trusts, and more. You need to make sure that your money is going to the people whom you've designated. Remember, a beneficiary designation supersedes whatever you state in your will. So no matter what your will says, the beneficiary designation will prevail.

Capital Gains

A capital gain is simply a profit you made when you sold an asset. Let's say you bought a stock for $2,000 and sold it for $8,000. In this case, your capital gain will be $6,000. Your net proceeds in this example are $8,000 and your cost basis (what you paid for it) is $2,000. The formula is as follows:

Net proceeds − cost basis = capital gain

The tax rate on a capital gain is much lower than on ordinary income. Capital gains are currently taxed at a 15 percent federal rate (plus whatever your state tax rate is), while ordinary income can be taxed up to a maximum of 35 percent (plus whatever your state tax rate is). You must hold an asset for at least twelve months in order to get this favorable 15 percent tax rate.

From there, it can get more complicated. For example, if you sell your primary residence, there is a capital gain exclusion of $250,000 per person, so if you're married, the exclusion is $500,000. Let's say you're married and you bought your house twenty-five years ago for $500,000 and sold it last year for $1,000,000. While your capital gain is $500,000 ($1,000,000 minus $500,000), your taxable gain is zero. That's because your married capital gain exclusion of $500,000 wipes out the capital gain.

However, if you owned a rental house, you don't get that capital gain exclusion benefit. On the flip side, with a rental house you're able to deduct depreciation from your income tax return every year. That's the good news. The bad news is each year that depreciation deduction reduces your cost basis, which will increase your capital gain when you sell it. In addition, all that accumulated depreciation is subject to a special 25 percent tax rate instead of the current 15 percent capital gains tax rate. If you're a real estate investor, you should read more about this in a white paper I wrote that is available on The Monitor Group website. It's called "Real Estate: A Tax and Investment Critique," and you can find it here: www.themonitorgroup.com/media/pdf/articles/taxplanning/02-08-Real-Estate-a-Tax-and-Investment-Critique.pdf.

Mutual funds (with reinvestment of dividends and capital gains distributions) and stock dividend reinvestment plans (DRIPs) create a benefit and a nightmare at the same time. When a dividend is reinvested in the mutual fund or stock, you pay income tax that year on that dividend, even though you did not receive it in cash. The good news is that you get to increase your cost basis. Otherwise, you'd be subject to double taxation—because you've already paid tax on the dividend, you shouldn't have to pay tax again on the amount that increased the value of your investment. The nightmare is tracking those increases in cost basis. Financial advisors and wealth managers use sophisticated technology to track cost basis, so when you sell a mutual fund or DRIP, you won't pay more tax than you should.

Cash Flow Plan and Monte Carlo Analysis

Cash Flow Illustration
Judy Sample

	Scheduled Cash flow sources and Required Minimum Distributions						Less Living Expense & Taxes	Surplus (Shortage)
Age	Earned Income	Retire/Roth Accounts *	Investment Accounts *	Pension/ SocSec	Other Income	Total Sources		
	1	2	3	4	5	6	7	8
40				$52,584		$52,584	($115,484)	($62,900)
41				53,636		53,636	(119,255)	(65,619)
42				54,708		54,708	(128,679)	(73,970)
43	60,000			33,316		93,316	(151,389)	(58,073)
44	61,800			33,682		95,482	(156,328)	(60,845)
45	63,654			34,047		97,701	(200,570)	(102,869)
46	65,564			34,409		99,973	(166,441)	(66,467)
47	67,531			34,770		102,301	(171,885)	(69,585)
48	69,556			35,128		104,684	(177,512)	(72,828)
49	71,643			35,483		107,126	(183,326)	(76,200)
50	73,792			35,834		109,626	(189,338)	(79,712)
51	76,006			36,182		112,188	(195,659)	(83,472)
52	78,286					78,286	(269,764)	(191,478)
53	80,635					80,635	(281,687)	(201,052)
54	83,054					83,054	(376,506)	(293,452)
55	85,546					85,546	(421,645)	(336,099)
56	88,112					88,112	(288,081)	(199,969)
57	90,755					90,755	(300,788)	(210,033)
58	93,478					93,478	(156,740)	(63,262)
59	96,282					96,282	(163,442)	(67,160)
60	99,171					99,171	(170,732)	(71,561)
61	102,146					102,146	(178,335)	(76,189)
62	105,210					105,210	(186,267)	(81,057)
63	108,367					108,367	(194,542)	(86,175)
64	111,618					111,618	(202,732)	(91,114)
65	114,966					114,966	(279,332)	(164,366)
66							(164,598)	(164,598)
67				51,289		51,289	(188,494)	(137,206)
68				52,314		52,314	(197,072)	(144,758)
69				53,361		53,361	(205,985)	(152,624)
70		411,095		54,428		465,523	(372,986)	92,537
71		441,923		55,516		497,439	(396,755)	100,684
72		475,023		56,627		531,650	(422,227)	109,423
73		510,557		57,759		568,316	(450,839)	117,478
74		548,698		58,914		607,612	(481,654)	125,958
75		589,628		60,093		649,721	(598,645)	51,076
76		633,540		61,295		694,835	(549,257)	145,578
77		677,431		62,520		739,951	(585,852)	154,100
78		727,711		63,771		791,482	(626,489)	164,993
79		777,604		65,046		842,650	(668,348)	174,302
80		830,620		66,347		896,967	(713,035)	183,932
81		886,905		67,674		954,579	(760,726)	193,854
82		946,600		69,028		1,015,628	(811,601)	204,026
83		1,009,840		70,408		1,080,248	(865,846)	214,402
84		1,076,747		71,816		1,148,563	(923,653)	224,911
85		1,139,674		73,253		1,212,927	(981,849)	231,077
86		1,205,202		74,718		1,279,920	(1,043,398)	236,521
87		1,273,237		76,212		1,349,449	(1,108,420)	241,029
88		1,343,637		77,736		1,421,373	(1,177,017)	244,356
89		1,416,188		79,291		1,495,479	(1,249,273)	246,206
90		1,477,519		80,877		1,558,396	(1,319,571)	238,825
91		1,538,699		82,494		1,621,193	(1,392,834)	228,360
92		1,599,146		84,144		1,683,290	(1,468,999)	214,291
	B9	C10, C11a	C4, C8	B10	B12, B12a		B8	

* Scheduled distributions, interest or dividends taken in cash or amounts taken to meet the IRS minimum distribution requirements.

Monte Carlo

Judy Sample

Monte Carlo Simulation illustrates possible variations in growth and/or depletion of retirement capital under unpredictable future conditions. The simulation introduces uncertainty by fluctuating annual rates of return on assets. The graph and related calculations do not presuppose or analyze any particular investment or investment strategy. This long-term hypothetical model is used to help show potential effects of market volatility and possible effects on your financial future. This is not a projection, but an illustration of uncertainty.

The simulations begin in the current year and model potential asset level changes over time. Included are all capital assets, both tax advantaged and taxable, all expenses, including education funding if applicable, pension benefits and Social Security benefits. Observing results from these large number of simulations may offer insight into the shape, trends and potential range of future retirement plan outcomes under volatile market conditions.

Results from 10,000 Monte Carlo Simulations:

Original Retirement Capital estimate	$88,059,694	**Percentage of results above zero***	81%
Minimum (worst case) result	$0	Percentage with $ remaining at Judy's age 87	87%
Average Monte Carlo result	$85,437,554	Percentage with $ remaining at Judy's age 82	93%
Maximum Monte Carlo result	$1,799,813,935	Percentage with $ remaining at Judy's age 77	97%
		Percent of times money is remaining at last age shown.	

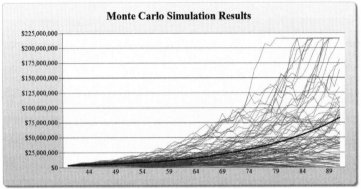

Monte Carlo Simulation Results

The bold line is the estimated retirement capital value over time using fixed rates.
Annual rate of return of 7.59% in the original retirement estimate varied from 7.59% to 7.89% based on portfolio changes over time.
This simulation used a 12.50% standard deviation to create ten thousand sets of normally distributed random rates of return
based on the annual rates of return in the original estimate (95% of the rates fall between -17.41% and 32.89%).
A standard deviation rate of 2.00% was applied to the inflation rate used on personal expenses.

The original capital estimate indicated a possibility of having $88,059,694 in assets remaining at last life expectancy. Monte Carlo simulation, using 10,000 trials of the same assets, income and expenses, resulted in a 81% probability of having funds remaining at last life expectancy, and an average amount of $85,437,554 remainin

The Monte Carlo illustration above points out the uncertainty of future retirement capital outcomes.
It is important that you return regularly for a review of your goals and financial condition, in order
to assure that appropriate periodic adjustments are made to your financial affairs.

IMPORTANT: The projections or other information generated in this report regarding the likelihood of various investment outcomes are hypothetical in nature, do not reflect actual investment products or results and are not guarantees of future results. Results may vary with each report and over time. Results of this simulation are neither guarantees nor projections of future results. Information is for illustrative purposes only. Do not rely on this report to predict actual performance of any investment or investment strategy.

De Minimus

If the probate estate is small, most states have a "de minimus" rule, which allows for a simplified and expedited probate process. For example, in Virginia, if the total value of the estate is $15,000 or less, no formal administration is necessary. In addition, the automobile owned by the deceased can be retitled without qualification. The will is simply recorded and nothing further is required. Different states have different rules and terms for handling small probate estates.

Diet

I like the South Beach Diet by cardiologist Arthur Agatston, MD, but my cardiologist prefers the Mediterranean Diet, found at www.mediterraneandiet.com. Another excellent program is the Duke Diet that was developed by experts at Duke University. To find out more, visit www.dukediet.com/kithe.aspx—a warning, the Duke program is expensive.

In addition, nationwide weight loss programs definitely produce results, and if you want or need accountability and face-to-face counseling, consider Weight Watchers, Jenny Craig, or Nutrisystem. Yes, you have to buy their prepackaged products, but you've got to buy food anyway, so that's really not a problem (unless you just don't like the taste of their food). Let's face it, any reasonable weight loss or nutrition plan will work if you just do it and keep doing it.

This is the secret I have finally figured out: "different strokes for different folks." We all have different personalities, preferences, tastes, and time commitments. So we need to discover the diet that will suit our individual profile. Frankly there are some things we will do, and keep doing, and there are others we won't. You have to experiment with different diets and discover the one that you will enjoy and continue to be faithful to without trying to be someone you're not. The same holds true for exercise.

There are now apps for smartphones that enable you to keep track of your calorie intake, walking distance, and other fitness and nutrition data. Personally I have benefited from using the app My Fitness Pal and its website www.myfitnesspal.com.

Disability Income Insurance

If you cannot work due to illness or injury, your income from your job will stop. So how will you pay your mortgage and your other bills? Disability income insurance provides you a monthly income in the event that you're unable to work. It is very important coverage to have throughout your working years. You should have a minimum of 60 percent of your annual income protected by disability income insurance.

You do have to buy this product from a commission-based financial advisor or an insurance salesperson, so make sure you're dealing with someone reputable. There are a lot of confusing terms and conditions. Here are the essentials:

- **Waiting (or elimination) period:** This is the number of days you have to wait after you become disabled before the policy starts paying your monthly benefit. The waiting period could be as short as ninety days or as long as a year. The longer the waiting period, the less the policy will cost you; that is, it has a lower premium.

- **Monthly benefit:** This is how much the policy will pay you each month as long as you meet its definition of disability. This benefit is tax-free if you paid for the policy out of your pocket. However, if you have a group disability policy through your employer, and your company pays the premiums, the benefit will be taxable income to you. In that case, you might want to supplement your group coverage with an individual policy. This is especially true if your income is in excess of $100,000 per year because most group policies cap their benefit at $5,000 per month (which is 60 percent of $100,000).

- **Two definitions of disability:** "Any occupation" and "own occupation." The difference between the two is tricky to decipher. Overall, "own occupation" is much better, but it will cost extra. If you have the "any occupation" definition, the policy will not pay disability benefits if you are able to work at any job. In other words, you have to be so disabled that you can't work anywhere doing anything. If you have the "own occupation" option, benefits will be paid if you cannot perform the functions of your current job, even though you may be working in another job.

- **Residual or partial disability:** What if you're not totally disabled, but because of serious back pain you can only work, say, for four hours a day? Would you collect half of your disability benefit? After all, theoretically your income would be cut approximately in half. The answer is a firm no! That is, unless you purchase an option, which the insurance industry calls a rider, that provides residual benefits. If you have a residual rider, you would collect the same percentage of your benefit as the percentage of your lost income. So if you lost 50 percent of your income, your monthly disability benefit would be 50 percent of the benefit you had purchased.

- **Cost of Living Adjustment (COLA):** If you purchase this rider, your monthly benefit will increase based on the increase in the Consumer Price Index or some other inflationary statistic as stated in the policy. This is tricky too. COLA will only start to increase after you become disabled and begin collecting benefits. Prior to becoming disabled, your benefit will not increase. The way to make sure your benefit increases with inflation prior to any disability is to purchase an additional insurance amount annually; many companies allow you to automatically buy a small additional amount each year without proving you're still healthy. Yes, this will increase your premium, but you won't be negatively surprised after you start collecting benefits.

- **Benefit period:** This is how many years your policy will pay your monthly benefit. You can buy a policy that will pay benefits for five years, ten years, to age sixty-five, or for the rest of your life. Obviously the longer the benefit period, the more your premium will cost. I recommend that my clients get nothing shorter than "to age sixty-five."

Diversification

See **asset allocation.**

Durable Power of Attorney

The words "power of attorney" mean that the person you name as "attorney-in-fact" or your "agent" has the legal authority to do anything you can do. The word "durable" means that it is in effect at any time. In general, a power of attorney creates an agency relationship where you delegate to another the authority to make decisions for you during your lifetime. For a more in-depth explanation, see chapter 1.

Estate Tax

Also popularly (or unpopularly) known as the death tax, the estate tax is imposed on the value of the gross estate of someone who dies. For the years 2011 and 2012, each person has a federal (IRS) exemption of $5 million, and a married couple has an exemption of $10 million. The amount over the exemption is taxed at a rate of 35 percent.

Some states impose an estate tax with a much lower exemption amount. For example, Maryland and the District of Columbia have a $1 million exemption. Any amount over that exemption is subject to a 16 percent state estate tax. To stay in compliance with the law, you should check your state's estate tax rules.

There are numerous legal strategies that are quite effective in minimizing or completely eliminating the estate tax. If you have a net worth in excess of $1 million, you should consult with an estate planning attorney or wealth manager (a financial advisor who works with wealthy families). He or she will help you devise strategies that will help meet your objectives.

Exercise

While a commercial diet plan will almost always cost you money, you can spend a lot or nothing at all when it comes to exercise. It can be as simple as following the example of Herschel Walker, the former pro football player. He claims that his entire exercise routine is comprised of thousands of push-ups and sit-ups a day. In addition, consider regular walks in your neighborhood, in malls, or on treadmills for a minimum of twenty minutes daily or at least three days per week. You can do push-ups, sit-ups, and walk for free! Keep in mind that a combination of cardio and light weights (resistance) is essential to a good exercise program. Certain types of yoga combine both of these.

You can join a gym or fitness center if, and only if, you will be disciplined and go several times a week consistently. Otherwise, as a financial advisor I advise you against the investment because you're just throwing money down the drain. If paying a monthly membership to have a facility to visit is the motivation you need to stay fit, then so be it. You can also set up an excellent exercise program in your home if you have any space at all. In my case, I just use a couple of dumbbells for weights and a treadmill for walking.

At the other end of the spectrum, for an intense program that really works, try P90X. You may have seen their infomercials on TV. In fact, the dumbbell program I use was developed by the same trainer who developed P90X. To check out their products and programs, go to www.beachbody.com.

Hiring a personal trainer is another option. While quite a bit more expensive, a trainer provides both accountability (so you'll keep at it) and professional knowledge (so you'll be doing the right exercises). As in the case of any form of diet and exercise, consult your doctor first if you're uncertain of any medical condition you may have or how to start.

Fair Market Value

The following is the classic definition of fair market value:

> *The price at which property would exchange hands between a willing buyer and a willing seller when the former is under no compulsion to buy and the latter is under no compulsion to sell, and both parties have reasonable knowledge of all relevant facts.*

A "marketable security" such as a stock, bond, or mutual fund that is traded on an exchange fits this definition. Home sales, on the other hand, are more difficult, but real estate appraisers and salespeople can determine a fairly accurate fair market value of a house based on comparable sales in the area, prices per square foot, and prices for land in the area. Determining fair market value for some assets is more complicated; these would include a partnership or a business.

It's important to come up with a fair market value of a deceased person's assets. This will allow the assets to be properly distributed to the heirs and beneficiaries according to the decedent's trust or will. It's also critical to determine the gross estate amount in order to calculate the federal or state estate tax. In complex situations, people often hire professionals, called appraisers and valuation experts, whose job is to determine the fair market value of assets.

Fee-Only Financial Advisor

Fee-only financial advisors do not sell any products. Period. A large percentage of financial advisors (well over 50 percent) are either paid by commission or through a combination of fee and commission. Financial advisors who work on commission make money when they sell you a product. Examples of products include insurance (all types), annuities, load mutual funds (front-end load or back-end load), and even stocks and bonds. Financial advisors who sell products on commission have a conflict of interest. Are they selling you something because it's best for you or because it gives them the highest commission? Commission advisors are agents for the company whose products they sell. This means that their primary loyalty is to their company, not their clients.

A fee and commission financial advisor sells products on commission and also has a fee option (usually for larger accounts). This hybrid role makes it appear as if they are fee-only advisors, but it's important to identify how they are charging their clients. In many cases, there are multiple layers of fees—the advisor's fee plus the fees of the investment managers who are managing your money. Many times this can be 2 percent to 3 percent of your account's assets a year. These advisors usually call their compensation "fee-based" as opposed to fee-only.

I used to be a fee and commission advisor, so I know the conflicts they deal with on a daily basis. It's a struggle to do the right thing for your client, particularly when it's in opposition to the possibility to make money for yourself. The conflict never goes away. This puts the client and the advisor in adversarial positions—clients are never sure if their advisors have their best interests at heart.

There are also fee-only financial advisors. These are fiduciaries. This means that by law (and by regulations of the SEC), they must put their clients' interests first. In fact, clients can sue a fiduciary if they believe that he or she did not act in their best interest. Note that the fiduciary standard doesn't apply to commission advisors. A fee-only advisor charges either a flat fee or a percentage of the assets under management (usually 1 percent per year or less). This arrangement puts the client and the advisor on the same side of the table—if the account value goes up, the clients are happy; their advisors are happy as well because their fee revenue increases as the account value climbs.

Commission advisors, on the other hand, get paid regardless of whether the account does well. They earn commissions when money is moved from one account to another, which means that they get paid on transactions, not on value. Therefore, there's an incentive to constantly move money from one investment to another. It may appear that they're "doing something" in trying to time the market or pick stocks. As I pointed out in chapter 5, such strategies rarely work. So, yes, they're often doing something all right—they're moving money from your account to theirs!

The main drawback with fee-only financial advisors is that they usually have high investment requirements. For example, my firm has a $1 million investment minimum. Other fee-only advisors I know have lower minimums, such as $500,000 or $250,000. Although the account minimum is high at The Monitor Group, we do not charge for additional services such as estate planning, financial projections, or tax planning. Some fee-only financial advisors charge extra for these additional services. You have to ask, and by law they should be up-front in disclosing all that information to you.

FEPA

FEPA is an acronym for formal estate planning analysis. It's a proprietary process we developed at The Monitor Group. FEPA takes the most important aspects of a client's estate and ensures that it is up to date and meets the overall objectives of a financial plan. As a result of FEPA, our clients have resolved legal and technical problems that could have been financially and emotionally disastrous. For example, FEPA reviews wills and trusts using diagnostic questions. These are designed to find potential problems that could cause significant problems for surviving family members in the future. FEPA ensures that a client's beneficiary designations for certain assets are exactly the people to whom they want to give this money (over time, things change through death, divorces, and strained relationships). These assets include IRAs, company retirement plans, life insurance, and more. In addition, FEPA reviews long-term care insurance and homeowners', auto, and umbrella insurance and makes sure that coverage meets a client's current needs. FEPA also includes customized checklists that clients give to their next of kin. These documents outline precisely what the executor and trustee must know in the event that a client becomes incapacitated or dies. Finally, FEPA identifies which parts of a client's financial plan require improvement or modification. FEPA is the most comprehensive estate plan analysis that I am aware of. I don't know of any other firm that takes such comprehensive preventive action.

General Money Management Tips

Clients regularly ask me for recommendations on money management basics. Here are some FAQs.

How do I keep track of spending and investments?
Use Microsoft Excel spreadsheets to set up different categories of spending (auto, food, housing, etc.) and have columns for each month. An alternative that I prefer is to use money management software like Quicken or Mint (www.mint.com) to record income and expenses for all your accounts.

How should I prepare my taxes?
For complex situations, you should meet with a professional tax advisor. For simple returns, here are three resources:
- IRS Free File site, www.irs.gov/freefile
- TurboTax from the makers of Quicken, www.turbotax.intuit.com
- TaxACT, www.taxact.com

How do I learn to take control of my finances?
Read *Total Money Makeover* by Dave Ramsey (www.daveramsey.com). It's a powerful book that provides straightforward

money management advice, and there are plenty of real-world examples.

Geriatric Care Manager

A professional geriatric care manager (GCM) is a health and human services specialist who helps families who are caring for older relatives. The GCM is trained and experienced in any of several fields related to care management, including nursing, gerontology, social work, and psychology. He or she also specializes in issues related to aging and elder care.

The GCM assists older adults and those with disabilities in attaining their maximum functional potential. In addition, the geriatric care manager is an experienced guide and resource for families of older adults and others with chronic needs, including helping those suffering from Alzheimer's or Parkinson's, or exhibiting symptoms of dementia.

The National Association of Professional Geriatric Care Managers (NAPGCM) is an organization of practitioners whose goal is the advancement of expert assistance to the elderly and their families. You can find a care manager by going to their website: www.caremanager.org.

Gerontologists are health-care professionals who specialize in helping people in nursing homes, senior citizen centers, and other similar facilities. There are several different types of gerontologists. These professionals may have degrees or training in nursing, psychology, sociology, or other social services-related professions. Gerontologists are also responsible for educating older people by giving informative presentations, publishing books and articles that pertain to the elderly population, and producing relevant films and television programs. For more information, refer to this website: www.gerontologist.com.

Guides to Retirement Living

Where I work, the local publication is called the Source Book. It's distributed three times a year and covers Delaware, Pennsylvania, New Jersey, the District of Columbia, Maryland, and Virginia. You can receive it free from www.retirement-living.com.

RetirementHomes.com (www.retirementhomes.com) provides information on retirement living options in all fifty states. Also, U.S. News & World Report has published rankings for fifteen thousand nursing homes called "U.S. News Best Nursing Homes." Each retirement home is ranked in three separate categories. Eighteen earned perfect scores. Each time a facility receives this rating, it is boosted to the Honor Roll. U.S. News & World Report's online records are updated every quarter using Medicare, Medicaid, and other government statistics. Visit www.health.usnews.com/senior-housing.

In addition, the US Department of Health and Human Services provides an online eldercare locator service at www.eldercare.gov/Eldercare.NET/Public/Index.aspx.

Once you've narrowed your search, the best way to finalize your retirement facility decision is to visit each potential residence. Once there, ask questions and observe the residents and staff to determine if the site is appropriate for your family member.

Health-Care Power of Attorney
See **advance medical directive.**

Investment Choices
The following explanations of investment choices are excerpts from the "Beginners' Guide to Asset Allocation, Diversification, and Rebalancing," a free publication presented online by the US

Securities and Exchange Commission (SEC), which regulates financial institutions:

> *. . . you should know that a vast array of investment products exists—including stocks and stock mutual funds, corporate and municipal bonds, bond mutual funds, lifecycle funds, exchange-traded funds, money market funds, and US Treasury securities. For many financial goals, investing in a mix of stocks, bonds, and cash can be a good strategy. Let's take a closer look at the characteristics of the three major asset categories.*

> ***Stocks*** *have historically had the greatest risk and highest returns among the three major asset categories. As an asset category, stocks are a portfolio's "heavy hitter," offering the greatest potential for growth. Stocks hit home runs but also strike out. The volatility of stocks makes them a very risky investment in the short-term. . . .*

> ***Bonds*** *are generally less volatile than stocks but offer more modest returns. As a result, an investor approaching a financial goal might increase his or her bond holdings relative to his or her stock holdings because the reduced risk of holding more bonds would be attractive to the investor despite their lower potential for growth. You should keep in mind that certain categories of bonds offer high returns similar to stocks. But these bonds, known as high-yield or junk bonds, also carry higher risk.*

> ***Cash and cash equivalents***—*such as savings deposits, certificates of deposit, treasury bills, money market*

deposit accounts, and money market funds—are the safest investments, but offer the lowest return of the three major asset categories. The chances of losing money on an investment in this asset category are generally extremely low. The federal government guarantees many investments in cash equivalents. Investment losses in non-guaranteed cash equivalents do occur, but infrequently. The primary concern for investors investing in cash equivalents is inflation risk. This is the risk that inflation will outpace and erode investment returns over time.

. . . These are the asset categories you would likely choose from when investing in a retirement savings program or a college savings plan. But other asset categories—including real estate, precious metals and other commodities, and private equity—also exist, and some investors may include these asset categories within a portfolio. Investments in these asset categories typically have category-specific risks. Before you make any investment, you should understand the risks of the investment and make sure the risks are appropriate for you.

For the remainder of this guide, visit www.sec.gov/investor/pubs/assetallocation.htm.

See also **asset allocation, modern portfolio theory, mutual fund, portfolio, rebalancing, risk versus reward,** and **stock selection.**

Irrevocable Trust

This type of trust cannot be changed. A revocable trust becomes irrevocable when the grantor (the person who created the trust) dies. An irrevocable trust is a separate "person" in the eyes of the government, including the IRS—it must file its own separate income tax return each year and has its own tax ID number (similar to a Social Security number).

It's possible to set up an irrevocable trust during a person's lifetime. Property contributed to such a trust is considered a taxable gift, subject to the gift tax rules in effect in that year. In 2011, there is a $13,000 gift tax exclusion (meaning no tax on gifts of that amount or less), plus a lifetime exclusion of $5 million. Note that any gift amounts above $13,000 will reduce the ultimate estate tax exemption, which, in 2011 and 2012, is also $5 million.

You give up control when you put assets into an irrevocable trust, so it should be taken very seriously. You should consider all the pros and cons. One of the big advantages of an irrevocable trust is asset protection. As long as the gift to the trust was not a "fraudulent conveyance" (that is, done in anticipation of a lawsuit or a creditor seeking to collect from you), once assets are placed in the trust, they are protected from creditors, ex-spouses, lawsuits, etc. Some states, such as Delaware and Alaska, have special provisions that give even greater asset protection.

Another advantage of an irrevocable trust is known as an "asset freeze." The value of the gift is frozen for estate tax purposes in the year that it was gifted to the trust. Any future appreciation in the value of the asset grows tax-free (for estate tax purposes). For example, if a piece of real estate valued at $5 million was gifted to an irrevocable trust in 2011, and it grew to $100 million by the time the grantor died, the beneficiaries of the trust could get that property at zero estate tax. Of course, any other assets the deceased owned at the time of his death would be subject to estate tax because he had used up his $5 million exemption amount.

An **irrevocable life insurance trust** (ILIT) can be an effective and inexpensive way to minimize estate taxes. It removes the face amount (death benefit) of the individual's life insurance policy from the taxable gross estate. The policy can be either transferred into the ILIT or purchased by the ILIT. If there is a transfer, there is a three-year look-back period in order for this strategy to work. In other words, if the person dies within three years of the transfer, the value of the life insurance death benefit will be brought back into the taxable gross estate.

See also **revocable living trust** and **testamentary trust**.

Life Insurance

Life insurance is both simple and very complex. The product itself is straightforward enough—if the insured person dies, then someone else (called the beneficiary) receives cash in the amount stipulated in the life insurance contract. This assumes that the insured has paid the cost (the premiums) for the insurance.

From a tax perspective, here are the benefits and drawbacks:

	Life insurance benefit	Life insurance drawback
Income tax	Life insurance proceeds (cash paid to the beneficiary) are income tax–free.	Premiums paid for coverage aren't usually tax deductible.
Estate tax	If and only if the policy is owned by an irrevocable trust or another person (such as a child), the death benefit will not increase estate taxes.	If owned by the deceased, life insurance proceeds are included in the taxable estate of the insured (the person who died). Thus, a large life insurance policy can increase the family's estate tax.

From there it gets very complicated. There are numerous life insurance products such as term, group term, level term, decreasing term, whole life, universal life, variable universal life, and various hybrids. Also, there's jargon such as paid-up additions, dividends, loans, cash value, surrender value, and others. In addition, there are strategies like buy–sell, split dollar, reverse split dollar, and key man. I will spare you the gory details of all this life insurance–speak and just concentrate on two major types—term and permanent.

Term life insurance is based on a simple premise: as you get older, you're more likely to die. The most basic form of term is called **annual renewal term**. This type of coverage gets more expensive every year. In addition, the older you get, the faster the costs increase each year.

In general, term is the least expensive life insurance. As you get older, however, it becomes much more expensive, and in your later years it can become cost prohibitive. In fact, for people who live into their eighties and nineties, it usually becomes too costly to keep. As a result, policyholders often cancel their coverage. This is the disadvantage of term insurance. In fact, it may surprise you to hear that very few death benefits are ever paid out for term insurance. One industry study placed the percentage as low as 1 percent. The low likelihood of payout is another factor that allows term insurance to be relatively inexpensive.

Permanent insurance is also called whole life, universal life, and more. The objective of this type of insurance is to average out the cost of coverage over your lifetime. Thus you pay more than what a term insurance policy would cost when you're younger but less than term when you're older. It is even possible to have a "paid up" policy, which means you have contributed so much to the policy that you don't owe any more premiums after a certain point.

In your younger years, when you're paying more—often much more—than the equivalent amount that a term policy would cost that year, the difference goes into a savings account inside the policy, which is called cash value. In addition, there are other administrative costs, which, depending on the company and the policy, can either be reasonable or ridiculously high. This of course reduces the amount that ends up in cash value. Over time the cash value earns interest (also called dividends).

The advantage of permanent coverage is that if you pay all the premiums on time, the policy should never lapse (that is, expire before you do). Thus the terms "whole life" and "permanent."

Living Will
See **advance medical directive.**

Marital Assets
Determining marital assets is important when dividing assets in a divorce settlement. Marital assets are all property acquired during the course of the marriage, regardless of ownership or who holds the title to it. Examples of marital assets include real estate, cash, stocks, bonds, mutual funds, IRAs and retirement accounts, cars, pensions, and insurance. Most courts also treat the increase in value after marriage of a premarital asset as a marital asset. If you owned an asset prior to marriage and continued to own it separately in your own name (or your own revocable trust), it would generally not be considered a marital asset.

In community property states (Arizona, California, Idaho, Louisiana, Nevada, New Mexico, Texas, Washington, and

Wisconsin), assets are categorized as separate property and are not marital assets if they fit any of the following criteria:

- They were acquired before marriage
- They were acquired by inheritance
- They were a gift
- They consist of assets traceable to other separate property, such as money received from the sale of a house owned before marriage
- The spouses agree they are separate property

You should consult a family law attorney for clarification regarding your particular circumstances.

Medicaid

Medicaid is not health insurance, but Medicare is. Rather, Medicaid is a poverty program. The fastest-growing aspect of Medicaid is nursing home coverage for people with low incomes and those who have "spent down" most of their assets. Like Medicare, Medicaid was signed into law in 1965. Although it is a federal program, it is administered by individual states.

Medicaid will pay for all nursing home costs, but all of your income (Social Security, pension, etc.) will have to first go to the government, except for $66 per month that you're allowed to keep. Medicaid does not pay you. Instead it pays the nursing home (or other health-care provider) directly.

How does one become eligible (that is, impoverished enough) for Medicaid? How much do you have to spend down your assets? There is not one clear answer to those questions because it is a joint federal–state program, and the rules change from state to state. To complicate matters further, the rules are constantly changing.

Many people mistakenly think they can give away their assets to their family members or to a trust and thus qualify for Medicaid. There are several problems with this. First, there is a five-year "look-back" period—this means the state will look back to see if you have given away any assets in the five years prior to filing for Medicaid. If you have, they will penalize you by forcing the family to pay for part or all of the nursing home costs based on a formula that includes how much was given away and the average cost of nursing home care in the state.

The look-back period determines which gifts or transfers will be subject to a penalty period, the length of which depends on the amount transferred. The penalty period is determined by dividing the amount transferred by the average monthly cost of nursing home care in the state. For instance, if the nursing home resident transferred $100,000 in a state where the average monthly cost of care was $5,000, the penalty period would be twenty months ($100,000/$5,000 = 20). Thus, the family would have to pay the full cost of nursing home care for twenty months.

Second, Medicaid does not recognize the gift tax exclusion of $13,000 per person per year; any and all gifts are subject to the look back. Third, it is illegal to defraud the Medicaid system, and you could go to jail. In fact, if lawyers or financial planners suggest that you do improper Medicaid planning, they could go to jail. This should not be taken lightly.

With that said, there may be some things you can do. Here are some strategies according to the website Elder Law Answers: www.elderlawanswers.com/Elder_Info/Elder_Article.asp?id=701.

The house is a protected asset for the spouse, if you have one. However, after you (or your spouse, if applicable) die, the state will seek to recover what it has spent on the nursing home from your estate, and the house is part of your estate. You could protect your house from this by establishing a "life estate" for the house, in which you give title to the house to one of your children, but you retain the right to live in the house for the rest of your life.

In this case, the house would not go through probate and would not be subject to the look back of Medicaid. You would have to establish the life estate and transfer the deed five years or more before you apply for Medicaid. Another strategy is to establish an irrevocable trust and transfer the house into it, again more than five years before you apply for Medicaid.

> *Applicants for Medicaid and their spouses may protect savings by spending them on noncountable assets. These expenditures may include:*
> - *Prepaying funeral expenses*
> - *Paying off a mortgage*
> - *Making repairs to a home*
> - *Replacing an old automobile*
> - *Updating home furnishings*
> - *Paying for more care at home*
> - *Buying a new home*
>
> *In the case of married couples, it is often important that any spend-down steps be taken only after the unhealthy spouse moves to a nursing home if this would affect the community spouse's resource allowance.*

Finally, this may be the one case where the purchase of an immediate annuity might make sense. Consult the Elder Law Answers website for details. The website is also a good referral souce for finding an attorney to help you in any of these areas.

Medicare

Medicare is a government-sponsored health insurance program that became the law of the land in 1965. This is the primary health insurance for all Americans age sixty-five years and older. You should apply for Medicare three months before your sixty-fifth birthday. If not, you may be assessed a penalty in the form of higher premiums that you may have to pay for the rest of your life.

Some disabled people under the age of sixty-five may also be eligible for Medicare. This is often the case if they are receiving Social Security disability benefits. Other specific medical conditions may also enable other individuals younger than age sixty-five to be eligible for Medicare.

A combination of payroll taxes (FICA and Medicare) and premiums paid by Medicare recipients finances the program. Part A of Medicare is free if you or your spouse has paid Medicare payroll taxes for at least ten years. If not, you will have to pay a premium for Part A. Everyone who opts for Part B must pay a premium. In 2011, it is at least $96.40 per month. Since 2007, however, if your income exceeds $85,000 for singles or $170,000 for couples, you must pay more.

Medicare has four parts:
- Part A—Hospital Coverage
- Part B—Medical Insurance
- Part C—Medicare Advantage Plans
- Part D—Prescription Drug Plans

As you might expect, just as with Part B there is an additional cost for Part C and Part D.

It would require another book to fully explain Medicare. If you or a loved one is nearing eligibility or is already eligible, you should refer to the official Medicare and Social Security websites, www.medicare.gov and www.ssa.gov, and gather as much information as you can. There's an overwhelming amount of information out there. Additionally, Wikipedia (www.wikipedia. org) has a solid explanation of Medicare and its various parts. You may also visit your local Social Security office and speak to a representative.

Modern Portfolio Theory

In 1952 Harry Markowitz wrote "Portfolio Selection" for his University of Chicago doctoral dissertation. That same year, his paper also appeared in the *Journal of Finance*. His thesis stated that a portfolio with a specific mix of investments would yield better results (higher return and lower risk) than a portfolio that was merely a collection of carefully selected stocks. This was a departure from the standard thinking of the time—still prevalent today—that says one should examine each investment separately. Markowitz proved that specific combinations of equity (stock) and fixed income (bond) investments could be allocated in a portfolio to produce the highest possible expected return with the lowest expected volatility. His work was the first to quantify the risk versus return trade-off. It also highlighted that there was an optimal curve (called the "efficient frontier") that contained the best combination of risk and return; that is, the highest return at a given level of risk.

The overall concepts in Markowitz's dissertation were dubbed "Modern Portfolio Theory." Thirty-eight years later, Markowitz was awarded the 1990 Nobel Prize in Economics along with William Sharpe and Merton Miller. Sharpe, who is currently a professor at Stanford, also developed the "Capital Asset Pricing Model" and the "Sharpe Ratio." The latter is a measure of return per unit of risk. These academics have profoundly shaped how institutional portfolios are managed. I recommend that my clients follow these experts' principles in managing their wealth.

See also **asset allocation, investment choices, mutual fund, portfolio, rebalancing, risk versus reward,** and **stock selection.**

Mutual Fund

A mutual fund is a company that brings together money from many people and invests it in stocks, bonds, or other assets. The mutual fund manager is a professional who invests the money according to a specific strategy or investment objective, which is defined in the prospectus. A prospectus is a legal document required by the SEC to be given to every potential investor in the mutual fund.

Advantages of a mutual fund include diversification, professional management, and liquidity. Liquidity means you can get your money out very quickly, usually within one day. A no-load fund has no penalty if you sell your fund (or a portion of it). A load fund may impose a sales charge if you sell within a specific period from the time you first purchased shares.

A money market fund is a type of mutual fund and is not guaranteed by the FDIC. A money market deposit account, however, is a bank product guaranteed by the FDIC up to $250,000 per account.

A disadvantage of mutual funds is that they invest in stocks, bonds, gold, or other investments that may go up or down in value on any given day, week, or year. If you sell when the price is down, you lose money. This is called a capital loss. The only good news about this is that you can deduct up to $3,000 per year of capital losses against other income on your tax return.

See also **asset allocation, investment choices, modern portfolio theory, portfolio, rebalancing, risk versus reward**, and **stock selection.**

Net Worth

Your net worth is the value of everything you own (your assets) minus everything you owe (also called your liabilities). If you've ever prepared a financial statement to get approved for a loan from a bank or mortgage company, you've had to calculate your net worth. Banks usually call it a financial statement.

In order to determine your assets, you add up all your bank accounts, investments, retirement plans, businesses, real estate, cars, and personal property. Then to calculate your liabilities, you'd combine all your credit card balances, car loans, mortgages, and other debts.

Subtract the liabilities from the assets and voilá—that's your net worth. A competent financial advisor will update your net worth statement at every meeting you have with him or her. Your net worth plus the death benefit of all life insurance you own is your gross estate, which is subject to estate tax. A well-developed net worth statement will also indicate whether each asset and liability is in the name of the husband or the wife, jointly owned, or in a revocable or irrevocable trust. All of these details are extremely important. It is also vital to balance the ownership of assets between spouses if possible—this can save on estate taxes.

Portfolio

By definition a portfolio is a collection. Just as an actor or model has a collection of photographs called a portfolio, your investment portfolio is the sum total of all your various investments. This could include bank accounts, stocks, mutual funds, real estate, and gold.

See also **asset allocation**, **investment choices**, **modern portfolio theory**, **mutual fund**, **rebalancing**, **risk versus reward**, and **stock selection.**

Probate

The word "probate" comes from a Latin word meaning "to prove." When someone dies, there is a legal process to prove what the person owned and owed, to whom the deceased's estate will be distributed, and what creditors have a legal right to collect. (An estate is everything the person owned—financial, real estate, personal property, etc.) This legal process takes place under the supervision of a probate court in the county in which the deceased was a resident. In addition, each state has its own laws that govern the technical steps and processes required in probate.

Whether or not the deceased had a will, the person's estate must be probated. As you've read in chapter 1, probate is no fun. The following are five reasons why:

- **Time:** It can take usually a minimum of six months and up to several years in order to complete the probate process; it usually takes longer if there is no will.
- **Money:** Any time you have to deal with the courts there is an expense involved. In some states, it doesn't cost much, while in other states, it can be very expensive. It may be necessary to pay the executor or administrator (also called a "personal representative") a fee to handle the probate process. For instance, in Florida, there are rules that almost always require you to hire a lawyer. In many states the probate court will require you to obtain a bond (meaning that you'll be responsible for buying

insurance) on the executor or administrator named in the will to protect against possible abuse by that person. This is usually true if the executor or administrator is from out of state. Finally, in many states it is necessary for the executor or administrator to file an accounting with the court on an annual basis as long as the probate estate is open. In some states, this may also be true if there is a "testamentary trust" (that is, a trust within the will), for as long as the testamentary trust is managing assets for its beneficiaries.

- **Publicity:** All wills are a matter of public record. If there is no will, the decision of the probate court is public as well.

- **Immediate distribution:** Once the probate process is complete, the assets are immediately distributed to the people named in the will. What happens if the heir is a child or a minor? Even if the heir is an adult, what if he or she is irresponsible? What if the spouse or the child is disabled or mentally incompetent—who will manage the assets in this case? What if there is a divorce between one or more of the heirs? What if there is the possibility of bankruptcy or other creditor problems with one or more of the heirs? A will is of no use in dealing with these issues. A trust, on the other hand, can handle them all very efficiently.

- **Wasting the estate tax credit:** There is a significant estate tax credit for each person. If the first spouse to die does not preserve his or her credit in a special "credit shelter trust," however, this credit can be wasted and can cost the heirs millions of dollars in needless estate taxes. This has been temporarily corrected by legislation signed by

President Obama in December 2010. The credit amount was increased to shelter $5 million of assets per person, and if a married person dies, his or her $5 million exemption is not wasted. However, this provision expires at the end of 2012 unless Congress extends it. Also, the growth on the $5 million of assets is not protected (as it would be in a credit shelter trust). In addition, the credit would be wasted if the surviving spouse remarries. It's complicated!

Ancillary probate is another concept you should be aware of. If you own property in more than one state—this usually applies to second homes or other real estate—and you die, your executor will have to deal with probate not only in your home state but also in all states in which you own property. Likewise, for property owned jointly with your spouse, if your spouse dies with you in a common accident or owns the property in his or her name solely after you die, your executor will have to deal with probate in all states where both of you own property. The only way around this is to title your out-of-state properties to a **revocable living trust** or to have it owned jointly with someone beside your spouse.

See also **net worth** and **testamentary trust.**

Rebalancing

In asset allocation, you establish target percentages for each asset category (also called asset class). For example, you might want to have 20 percent in short-term bonds, 20 percent in intermediate term bonds, 15 percent in large cap value stocks, 15 percent in large cap growth stocks, 10 percent in small cap value stocks, 10 percent in small cap growth stocks, and 10 percent in international stocks. In this example, you have 40 percent in bonds and 60 percent in stocks. Please keep in mind that these percentages are provided for illustrative purposes only; this is not a recommendation.

As the market ebbs and flows, your portfolio will get out of balance. For example, if stocks do well and bonds don't do as well, those percentages get out of whack. Rebalancing is the discipline of skimming off the profits of the asset classes that have done well and buying the asset classes that have not done as well.

In the above example, we had a target of 40 percent in bonds and 60 percent in stocks. If the stocks had gone up substantially, your unadjusted portfolio might be 30 percent in bonds and 70 percent in stocks. Without doing anything, your portfolio has become more risky. So it's time to rebalance. You would sell some of the stocks in order to get back to 60 percent, and you would buy bonds in order to get back to 40 percent.

That's a macro view. The micro view would be to look at each of the allocation percentages for all of the asset classes and do the rebalancing for each asset class. Small cap stocks may have gone up a lot, large cap stocks a little, and international stocks may have actually gone down in our fictitious scenario. So in rebalancing you would sell more of the small caps to get them back down to their 10 percent allocation and some of the large caps to get them back down to their 15 percent allocation, but you would buy some of the international stocks to get them back up to their 10 percent allocation.

While this example appears simple enough, it's actually counterintuitive and therefore it's emotionally difficult to pull the trigger. Why? Because you're selling the stuff that has been doing well and buying stuff that has been doing poorly! Most people would rather keep their winners and sell their losers, which is why individual investors usually perform so poorly (remember the DALBAR study in chapter 5?).

The objective, unemotional counsel of a fee-only financial advisor can make sure rebalancing happens. It's important to do this because what goes up will eventually come back down, and what goes down does not stay down. I'm speaking of broadly diversified asset class funds and not individual stocks. Individual stocks can go down and stay down (or the company can even go out of business). Another benefit of rebalancing is that it forces you to "buy low and sell high." When you rebalance, you skim off the profits of your winning asset classes, and you buy asset classes whose prices have gone down; so you're selling high and redeploying those profits by buying low.

See also **asset allocation, investment choices, modern portfolio theory, mutual fund, portfolio, risk versus reward,** and **stock selection.**

Revocable Living Trust

The word "revocable" means the document can be amended or changed at any time by the person who created the trust, who is also called the "grantor." A revocable trust does not have to file a separate tax return. All taxable income from assets in the trust (interest, dividends, rental income, capital gains, etc.) are taxed to the grantor's Social Security number, and filed on his or her personal 1040 tax return. Transfers of assets into a revocable trust are not taxable gifts.

The second word in revocable living trust—living—is important to note. This indicates that the trust was formed during the grantor's lifetime. Sometimes the Latin words inter vivos are used, which simply means "during life." An inter vivos trust is different from a "testamentary trust," which comes into being after the person's death as part of the decedent's last will and testament.

The trust document names a trustee, who has the responsibility to manage all assets titled to the trust. During the grantor's life, the grantor is typically also the trustee, often cotrustee with his or her spouse. Therefore, the grantor also manages the assets for his or her benefit, just as if there were no trust. The trustee has a "fiduciary" legal responsibility to act in the absolute best interests of the beneficiaries. There can be two types of beneficiaries: income and remainder. Income beneficiaries are entitled to annual income from the trust according to the terms of the document. Remainder beneficiaries receive the assets from the trust when the trust terminates or upon attaining certain ages or fulfilling certain responsibilities specified by the trust document.

Many institutions, such as banks and brokerages, will not accept a power of attorney, or they'll make it a major hassle to use one. A trust with a cotrustee or successor trustee, however, does not have these problems; they are readily accepted, and they can be used immediately without delay. While a living trust has this advantage, a testamentary trust does not for the simple reason that a testamentary trust does not come into being until after the person has died. It cannot spring into existence prior to death.

See also **irrevocable trust** and **testamentary trust**.

Risk versus Reward

When it comes to investing, risk and reward are inextricably entwined. You've probably heard the phrase "no pain, no gain." Those words come close to summing up the relationship between risk and reward. All investments involve a degree of risk—and don't let anyone tell you otherwise. If you plan to purchase securities—e.g., stocks, bonds, or mutual funds—it's imperative that you understand that you could lose some or all of your money.

The reward for taking on risk is the potential for a greater investment return. If you have a financial goal with a long time horizon, you are likely to make more money by carefully investing in asset categories with greater risk, like stocks or bonds, rather than restricting your investments to assets with less risk, like cash equivalents. On the other hand, investing solely in cash investments may be appropriate in order to meet short-term financial goals.

See also **asset allocation**, **investment choices**, **modern portfolio theory**, **mutual fund**, **portfolio**, **rebalancing**, and **stock selection.**

Stock Selection

Stock selection is the concept of picking stocks; that is, evaluating stocks of various companies according to a set of criteria and then deciding to buy the stocks that meet the particular criteria. Examples of criteria include the following:

- **Market capitalization**—Size of the company: large, medium, or small cap
- **Sector or industry**—Such as automobile, energy (oil or gas), and retail
- **Price**—Some people only buy stocks with low prices, such as those that are less than ten dollars per share
- **Dividend yield**—Similar to interest rate. To determine this, you calculate the percentage of the annual cash dividend per share divided by the stock price. For example, if General Electric is paying a quarterly dividend of 14

cents per share, that's 56 cents per share annually (4 x 14 = 56). If GE stock is trading at $20 per share, the dividend yield is 0.56/20 = 2.8 percent.

- **Dividend growth**—The company has consistently increased its dividend over many years
- **Analyst ratings**—You can buy what your favorite analysts or a combination of analysts recommend, or be a contrarian and buy what they don't recommend. The latter goes along with the mindset that so-called experts are usually wrong.
- **Revenue growth, earnings growth, or earnings surprises**
- **Momentum**—The price, revenue, earnings, or all of them combined seem to be on a continuing upward trend.
- **Beta**—A measure of the volatility of the stock compared to the stock market index.
- **Price/Earnings (P/E), Price/Book, Price/Sales or Price/Cash Flow ratios**—If the ratio is lower than average for the industry or the market, it may be a "value"; in other words, a good buy.
- **PEG Ratio**—The P/E ratio divided by the estimated growth rate of the company.
- **Moving average**—The price of the stock is above a 50-day or 200-day moving average of the price of the stock

That last one is called a "technical" indicator. All the previous ones are called "fundamental" indicators. Fundamental analysis looks at what a particular company is actually doing. Technical analysis isn't concerned with a company's activities, focusing instead on past performance data—usually price and volume—as well as volatility.

Although these stock selection criteria can become interesting to the point of near obsession, the bottom line is that they attempt to predict the unpredictable. That is, the future direction of the price of any stock is unknowable. No one can predict the future of anything, including stock prices. For some reason, however, the investing public seems to have a desperate need to believe that there are investing gurus who can.

See also **asset allocation, investment choices, modern portfolio theory, mutual fund, portfolio, rebalancing**, and **risk versus reward.**

Testamentary Trust

It's possible to have a trust within the will. This is called a testamentary trust (you've probably heard the term "last will and testament"). A testamentary trust can handle the problems of immediate distribution.

In some states, usually "community property" states, it is preferable to use a testamentary trust rather than a revocable living trust. This is due to a significant benefit to heirs in community property states; that is, all assets get a step-up in basis (even those of the surviving spouse). There is some legal question regarding whether the step-up in basis will be available if assets are titled to a trust during one's lifetime. In these states, many attorneys prefer testamentary trusts. A testamentary trust can also contain a credit shelter trust, so the estate tax credit of the first spouse to die is not wasted.

See also **irrevocable trust** and **revocable living trust.**

Titling and Registration

All assets are owned by someone or something. The owner has title to the asset. Titling is the act of assigning ownership to an asset. It may also be referred to as the registration on an account.

For example, if you own a house, you have title to the deed for that property. Put another way, the ownership of the house is registered to you. The registration may be joint; that is, titled to a husband and wife. In this instance, the registration may read: "John and Mary Smith, jointly owned as tenants by the entirety." The registration on a bank account may read "John and Mary Smith, joint tenants with rights of survivorship." The registration on a piece of real estate owned by two unrelated people may read "David Hill and Thomas Jones, joint tenants in common."

Proper titling is essential, as it determines who legally owns the property, which will in turn determine who gets the property when an owner (or one of the joint owners) dies. An investment account could be retitled from an individual's name to that individual's revocable living trust. Likewise, a life insurance policy could be titled to an irrevocable trust.

It's important to regularly review the titling of every asset you own. This will ensure that your assets pass according to your wishes. Remember, joint tenancy supersedes whatever your will says. That is, if you own any account or property jointly with rights of survivorship and you die, the asset will go to the joint owner and not to the person or organization that you stated in your will. On the other hand, anything titled jointly as "tenants in common" will pass according to your estate documents, such as the will or trust.

About the Author

Cal Brown, CFP®, MST
Vice President of Planning

Cal Brown has over twenty-five years of experience in the financial services field. He received his master of science in taxation (MST) from American University in Washington, DC, and his undergraduate BSBA degree from the University of Arkansas. Cal is currently an adjunct professor in the MST program at American University, teaching estate planning.

Washingtonian magazine and *Northern Virginia* magazine named Cal one of the top financial planners in the greater Washington, DC, metro area, and he has authored articles appearing in *Bloomberg Wealth Manager*, *Journal of Financial Planning*, and *Financial Planning* magazines. He has also been quoted in the *Wall Street Journal*, *Newsweek*, *U.S. News and World Report*, *Kiplinger's Personal Finance*, *Smart Money*, and other periodicals. He has appeared on CNBC, Fox 5 DC, the PBS *Nightly Business Report*, and was a regular guest on WAVA-FM (Washington, DC).

As a speaker, he has addressed national audiences as well as local and regional professional and civic groups. Cal served as chairman of the National Capital Area chapter of the Financial Planning Association and continues to actively serve on boards and councils within his profession.

Cal is vice president of planning for The Monitor Group in McLean, Virginia, a wealth management firm working with over 250 clients and managing approximately $500 million in assets.

Cal also plays guitar in a classic rock cover band in northern Virginia.